School Choice and the Quasi-market

Oxford
Educational Studies

·lons

·19

School Choice and the Quasi-market

Edited by Geoffrey Walford

*Oxford Studies in Comparative Education,
Volume 6(1)*

General Editor: David Phillips

Triangle Books
PO Box 65, Wallingford, Oxfordshire OX10 0YG, United Kingdom
Triangle Books is a division of Triangle Journals Ltd

Published in the United Kingdom, 1996
© Triangle Journals Ltd

ISBN 1 873927 23 1

**This publication is also available on a subscription basis
as Volume 6(1) of *Oxford Studies in Comparative Education*
(ISSN 0961-2149).**

Typeset in Monotype Plantin by Triangle Journals Ltd
Printed and bound in the United Kingdom by Cambridge University Press

Contents

School Choice and the Quasi-market

GEOFFREY WALFORD

Introduction

Throughout much of the industrialised world the 1980s saw governments divesting themselves of responsibility for designing, organising and providing services for their citizens. In country after country, the ideology of the market swept away ideas of rational planning, and massive privatisation programmes of state-owned manufacturing and service organisations have resulted. It is argued that greater use of market mechanisms not only helps to solve economic problems, but also contributes to the well-being of the population by allowing individuals greater freedom and control over their own lives. The market, it is argued, encourages the qualities of independence, self-reliance and self-respect which had been corroded by the workings of an all-powerful, interfering state. Moreover, the 'discipline of the market' is said to ensure that only high quality provision survives. Competition between suppliers is believed to raise the quality of products from all suppliers, and ensure that customers get good 'value for money'.

It was almost inevitable that such market thinking would be extended to the provision of schooling, and the 1980s and 1990s have seen many different countries radically reorganise their state-maintained schooling systems. This has often been accompanied by greater financial and ideological support for the private sector and a greater blurring of the distinction between private and state-maintained schooling. All schools have been pushed into a situation more resembling the competitive market. The official aims have usually been couched in terms of increasing the efficiency and effectiveness of schooling by introducing competition between schools. But in many cases the call for greater efficiency has actually masked declining government funding for schools and a resultant partial privatisation of the educational system. This has frequently led to greater inequalities between schools, and greater inequities in the educational experiences of children from different genders, social classes and ethnicities.

The extension of market ideas into education has not been without criticism, and there has been considerable debate about the effects and desirability of such moves. Many critics believe that education should be viewed as a public good and that it is a grave error to treat the provision of schooling as a marketable commodity (e.g. Wringe, 1994). In practice, all market-oriented schemes so far introduced have accepted this argument to some degree. The nature of the market introduced into education is not identical to that found in manufacturing or even in major service industries. It is generally recognised that the schooling of a society's young holds benefits for the individual, the family and the society itself, and all Western societies have legislated to ensure that children receive some education whether or not the family or child wishes.

The term 'quasi-market' (Le Grand, 1991; Glennerster, 1991; Le Grand & Bartlett, 1993) has been often used to describe the current situation. It indicates that the market forces introduced into schooling differ in some fundamental aspects from classical free markets both in respect of the demand and supply side. One essential difference is that money need not change hands between the 'purchaser' and the 'supplier'. A second, is that society forces all families to make some sort of purchase from what is already on offer, or convince those with power to enforce that the family is providing a similar 'product' itself. On the supply side, the institutions providing schooling are not necessarily privately owned or have profit maximization as their main objective. Further, entry of new suppliers is regulated and subject to strict controls. Consumers do not have the freedom to choose any product, but only products that have been deemed to meet relatively strongly defined and inspected criteria. On the demand side, the purchaser is not necessarily the 'consumer' of what schools offer and this particular quasi-market may be conceptualised in terms of a diversity of purchasers and consumers. More fundamentally, children realistically only have one chance of receiving basic schooling. If the wrong choice is made, the personal costs of changing schools are high. Moreover, the market forces introduced into schooling differ from those of the classical market in that the act of choosing can directly transform the product. Market forces in schooling lead to some schools becoming full while others are empty – a choice for a small school is made invalid if it expands to meet the demand (Carroll & Walford, 1996).

While the market for schools is actually a quasi-market, some of its effects may equal those of the classical market. In particular, differences between schools can develop, such that those families that value education begin to see schools within a local hierarchy of desirability. Those at the top of that hierarchy become highly popular for both families and teachers. As they are likely to become oversubscribed, they are thus able to select children and families rather than families choosing schools. As the article by Liz Gordon makes clear, New Zealand's virtual abolition of its educational system, as such, has led to a competitive jungle of autonomous suppliers of schooling. The result has been a deepening of the polarisations already evident in New Zealand society, as those families with cultural and financial capital fight to ensure that their offspring attend the schools perceived to be the 'best'. At the other extreme, some families find themselves locked into suppliers that are gradually facing going out of business. Some schools close as the result of families choosing not to use them, but the closure is rarely swift or efficient. The children within those schools often suffer years of staff demoralisation and declining quality of facilities provided. The quasi-market of schools is potentially not just hard on suppliers, but can directly effect those families and children who have been unlucky enough to have made an inappropriate purchase. There is no 'money back guarantee' with schooling.

While there are general trends that can be perceived in numerous Western countries, each system has responded to the push for greater market forces in a different way. To begin to understand the results of such changes, they need to be examined within their own particular socio-economic and historic context. When different countries are studied in detail considerable differences are found in, for example, the degree of regulation of the market, the extent of incorporation of the private sector, and the relationships between choice and competition. These can be related to the variety of different purposes that governments saw for such developments and the degree to which collective responsibility for public education is accepted. Once individual countries are examined sweeping generalizations about market changes need to be hedged by caveats. But the examination of such differences allows a far deeper understanding of the complexity of responses.

This issue of *Oxford Studies in Comparative Education* brings together accounts of developments in the quasi-market of schools in nine different countries. They are all specially written by scholars who have substantial experience of researching the effects of these changes. These authors were asked to focus on their own particular country and to review policy developments in school choice over the last five to ten years. In addition to this general review, authors were asked to assess the research evidence on the workings of the 'quasi-market' of schools and, in particular, the effects of such changes on children of different genders and from differing social class and ethnic backgrounds. The intention was also that it would be possible to cover some of the other related issues such as: the nature of the choice-making process; the relationship between parent/child choice and selection by schools; the connection between school choice programmes and broader government policy; the nature of resistance and contestation of policies; and the possible longer-term effects of the changes on education and schooling. It was recognised that the precise issues to be covered would depend on the country under consideration.

The scholars invited to contribute to this issue have responded to the challenge and have produced as series of new and thought-provoking articles. Together, they add greatly to our understanding of the pressures that led to quasi-markets in education, and of how particular countries have responded to such changes and to the potentially inequitable effects of such moves.

The Articles

The collection starts by considering two northern European countries which, in very different ways have been the focus of debate on school choice and the quasi-market. The Netherlands is an example where, for many decades, parents or other groups have been able to establish new schools relatively easily, and families have been able to use a school of their choice for their children. The article by Karsten & Teelken examines the accuracy of this picture. They show that the principle that parents should be given the opportunity to organise and choose the kind of education they want for their children has long been central to the Dutch education system. It was the result of an extended campaign which spanned the late 19th and early 20th centuries. In 1848 freedom of education was established by the Constitution, such that parents and others had the right to found schools, organise them and to determine the religious and other convictions on which they are based. These rights were realised in a material sense through the historic compromise which is known as the Pacification of 1917, after which private schools were supported by the state on an equal financial footing to state schools. This accounts for the present wide variety of (mainly denominational) schools, and the fact that the Netherlands now has a majority of schools that are private and run by independent boards.

The ease with which various groups could establish their own schools in the Netherlands has often been used as a reference point for both positive and negative arguments about choice elsewhere in the world – 'often with little factual basis' as Glenn (1989) pointed out. The problem with using the Dutch model in this way is that often little or no attention is paid to the specific socio-cultural setting that keeps the country's unique education policies in place (Walford, 1995). Even more important, it neglects the question as to whether the solution arrived at in the Dutch situation of 1917 is still appropriate in a contemporary context. Karsten & Teelken describe the relations which have developed historically, and the way the system of free school choice actually operates. They also indicate some of the present problems within the system and discuss some contemporary issues.

Gary Miron considers the contrasting case of Sweden. Long known for its emphasis on political consensus, central planning, and egalitarianism, Sweden has seen dramatic changes in the last decade. Within education, moves towards greater diversity were made in the late 1980s, but 1992 saw a 'free choice revolution' that required municipalities to distribute resources to both public and private schools based upon the specific needs of each school. Through a voucher system the municipalities were required to fund at least 85 per cent of the costs of average per-student cost in a state school for each student enrolled in approved private schools. This degree of public support for the private sector is one of the highest in the world. Miron traces the political and economic factors that led to these changes and documents the resulting growth of the private sector in Sweden over the 1990s. He then examines the types of school that families are choosing and the reasons that they give for their decisions. It is shown that, while Montessori schools have shown the greatest increase among the various private schools, religious schools have also rapidly increased and now account for around 16 per cent of enrolments in private schools.

One of the results of recent changes in Sweden is that concern has arisen about segregation by ethnic grouping, social class and ability level. While it is still too early in the reforms to have definitive evidence, within the larger urban areas there are indications of growing segregation and disparities between schools. One particular concern is that private schools are able to use high fees or entry tests to select a rather homogeneous group, while municipal schools are obliged to accept all children. In Stockholm and its surrounding municipalities children of Swedish origin are moving from schools which have a large number of immigrant children, while children of well-educated immigrants are starting to move from schools predominantly containing immigrants. These are just some of the negative consequences of recent changes, but Miron clarifies that the developments in choice have been accompanied by budget cuts and argues that many of the negative consequences are not necessarily due to school choice and the use of vouchers. Moreover, it is evident that the reforms have led to increased efficiency in municipal schools, and that the balance between efficiency, effectiveness and equity is not easily assessed.

In the next article Geoffrey Walford describes the introduction of a quasi-market for schools into England and Wales that occurred during the mid 1980s, and early 1990s. He traces how the concept of choice developed since the 1944 Education Act, and shows how it has been used to justify a range of changes within both the private and state-maintained sectors of schooling. He pays particular attention to the City Technology College policy which, although small and generally deemed to have failed, can be seen as the forerunner of greater changes in the late 1980s. These later changes allowed state-maintained schools to 'opt out' of the control of their local education authority and become grant maintained, and introduced local management of schools which, coupled with open enrolment and budgets based on pupil numbers, led to the possibility of a highly competitive and inequitable system. This possibility was amplified through further legislative changes in the early 1990s.

Walford reviews the research evidence on the workings of the new quasi-market system, paying particular attention to the research on how families choose particular schools and on the growing inequalities between schools. He argues that competition between schools is leading to a hierarchy of differentially supported schools which are beginning to serve particular social and cultural groups. While some children now find themselves in well-equipped and staffed schools, others are faced with a depressing environment and with poor facilities and little external support. The comprehensive system is being replaced by a variety of schools with new forms of selection. Moreover, the new criteria are less clear or equitable than those used to select children for grammar or secondary modern schools within the discredited bipartite system that preceded comprehensive reform.

The article by Agnès van Zanten shows that, within France, the private sector is a major consideration. The private sector is subsidized by the state and schools about fifteen per cent of the relevant population. Although largely nominally Catholic, many private schools play down their religious orientation and the sector thus offers schools with a diversity of ethos and educational styles. The broadly comprehensive system that gradually developed after the Second World War was subject to growing criticism and a form of limited school choice was implemented in the mid 1980s. About a half of all secondary schools are now part of a decentralization scheme where parents can choose schools from within wider catchment areas, and parents now have a greatly increased influence on their children's school careers.

Van Zanten examines the elements of the ideologies held by French parents about schooling, and describes the ways in which increased choice intervenes in this specific ideological configuration. Although the extent of choice remains modest compared with other countries, she shows that there is considerable variation between social classes, with the middle-class benefiting most from recent changes. Van Zanten argues that the ideal of the common school is being replaced by the ideal of the 'patterned' school geared towards the satisfaction of particular customers. She speculates about the possible effects of further marketization in French education, focusing, in particular, on the effects of increased segregation between different ethnic groups.

A detailed account of the characteristics of the quasi-market in Germany is given by Weiss & Steinert in the following article. It is shown that differentiation and hierarchy have long been a characteristic of German secondary schooling, but it is argued that the educational quasi-market mainly operates only in cities and urban conurbations. They document regional, gender, ethnic and social differences in educational participation and qualifications gained, and argue that recent changes may amplify these inequities. In particular, parents have recently been given greater freedom of choice. Traditionally, the authority to decide what type of secondary school their child attends legally rested with the parents, but, in practice, the recommendation of the primary school teacher has always played a major role in the parents' decision. Additionally, until recently, specific achievement requirements (an examination or a trial period of instruction) were necessary if – contrary to the primary school recommendation – parents wanted their child to attend a school leading to university entrance qualification (Abitur). A number of Länder have now revoked this requirement, thus giving parents the full authority over their child's school career, potentially leading to greater inequalities.

The development and effects of increased school choice in the United States is the subject of the article by Peter Cookson Jr. There, a diversity of school choice schemes have been introduced which range from vouchers which fund part of private school fees, to charter schools, and to wholesale privatisation of schools. First, Cookson outlines the current variety of schemes in action or planned and gives a summary of public opinion on school choice. Second, he provides an historical and theoretical framework for understanding why the deregulation and commercialization of public education has an appeal to so many policy-makers, politicians, and other agents of symbolic control. Next, there is an examination of the major choice plans in the United States that rely on market principles of organization, and a review of the most recent empirical evidence about the relationship of market reforms to student achievement. Finally, Cookson argues that market solutions to educational problems misdefine the purpose of education in a democracy, and warns that the dangers of mistaking the public good with the economic welfare of the already privileged, if not corrected, could destroy democratically controlled education.

In his article on Australia, Simon Marginson first describes the dual system of state and private schools. The private schools currently enrol nearly 30 per cent of all students, are heavily subsidised by government and enjoy strong community support. This has normalised markets in schooling, despite their limited capacity to provide for unfettered choice. Since the late 1980s, quasi-markets have been created in each of Australia's eight State and Territory systems of government schooling. The most profound changes have occurred in Victoria. Here the changes were preceded by dramatic cuts in expenditure, with 230 schools being closed and 8200 teaching positions being abolished. Over 500 special teaching positions allocated to schools experiencing socio-economic disadvantage were abolished, resources were switched from non-Anglo communities to middle-class white districts, and class size rose rapidly. These cuts and redistribution of expenditure were followed by a new reformed system characterised by devolution, competition, strong central controls and a growing reliance on fund-raising, commercial sponsorship and fees. Marginson argues that the changes have been so drastic that free education has almost disappeared.

There is growing evidence of a marked increase in the proportion of funding obtained from fees and commercial sponsorship. As might be expected, the capacity for schools to raise such income is differentiated along socio-economic lines, and resource inequalities between schools in different socio-economic zones are growing. Marginson argues that schools in Australia are now segmented between two kinds of schools. First, there are those that are exclusive to varying degrees, which include most private schools and some oversubscribed government schools. Second, there are those schools that are freely accessible to parental choice, and thus condemned to inferiority in their social standing and educational resources.

A very similar situation is reported by Liz Gordon in her article on the quasi-market in New Zealand. What was once one of the most centralised and social democratic systems of education in the world has recently been swept away. A system based on full comprehensive education, where it was assumed that, wherever people lived, they would have access to a school offering the same range of opportunities as any other school, was replaced in 1989. The Department of Education and all regional bodies were abolished. In their place was put a small, policy-focused ministry plus four stand alone agencies covering accountability, qualifications and assessment, special education and training. Each school was given a Board of Trustees and highly devolved powers and responsibilities. This policy was originally seen as having elements of 'community empowerment' as well as those of the market and privatisation; however, in the seven years since implementation it has become clear that the emphasis on the market has predominated.

Gordon shows that the market is underpinned by a particular conception of choice that emphasises 'exit' rather than 'voice'. Schools are funded almost entirely on the basis of student numbers, and so the primary driving force for schools in the quasi-market is maintaining and improving student numbers. She reviews the evidence and indicates that a key feature of the operation of the quasi-market in schools has been a polarisation in the market popularity of schools that is based on, but reinforces, growing societal trends in inequality between various social groups. Whilst the School Boards in the wealthy areas are able to attract highly experienced and skilled members, and to draw upon the cultural and financial capital of the neighbourhood for support, schools in poor areas had far less chance of being able to obtain such assistance. Further evidence shows that the patterns of school choice are directly related to the class and ethnic character of the area in which schools are located – leading to increased polarisation of populations, resources and positionings of schools.

The picture presented by Liz Gordon is similar to that given in many of the preceding articles. While the stated aim of school reform was frequently voiced in terms of improving the quality of education in all schools in the sate sector, there is little evidence that this is happening. Indeed, there is little evidence that competition *could* translate into school improvement. In contrast, there is growing evidence that the quasi-market of schools is leading to greater inequity between schools, and greater polarisation between various social and ethnic groups within each society. In many cases the quasi-market appears to be masking a desire to reduce public expenditure on schooling and introduce a process of gradual privatisation. If such a desire is allowed to come to fruition, the effects on those societies could be incalculable.

References

Carroll, S. & Walford, G. (1996) Parents' responses to the school quasi-market, *Research Papers in Education,* (forthcoming).

Glenn, C.L. (1989) *Choice of Schools in Six Nations.* Washington: US Government Printing Office.

Glennerster, H. (1991) Quasi-markets and education, *Economic Journal,* 101, pp. 1268-1271.

Le Grand, J. (1991) Quasi-markets and social policy, *Economic Journal,* 101, pp. 1256-1267.

Le Grand, J. & Bartlett, W. (1993) *Quasi-markets and Social Policy.* London: Macmillan.

Walford, G. (1995) Faith-based grant-maintained schools: selective international borrowing from the Netherlands, *Journal of Educational Policy,* 10, pp. 245-257.

Wringe, C. (1994) Markets, values and education, in D. Bridges & T.H. McLaughlin (Eds) *Education and the Market Place.* London: Falmer.

Oxford Studies in Comparative Education, Vol. 6(1), 1996

School Choice in
the Netherlands

SJOERD KARSTEN & CHRISTINE TEELKEN

Introduction

The principle that parents should be given the opportunity to organise and choose the kind of education they want has traditionally been central to the Dutch education system. A long campaign which spanned the late 19th and early 20th centuries was conducted under the slogan 'schools to the parents' and resulted in the historic compromise which is known as the Pacification of 1917. The compromise which was agreed was that from then on private schools were to be supported by the state on an equal financial footing to state schools.

In 1848 freedom of education was established in the Constitution. This threefold freedom – to found schools, organise them and to determine the religious and other convictions on which they are based – accounts for the present wide variety of (mainly denominational) schools. The principle of equal state support made it possible for this freedom to be realised in a material sense. The result has been that the Netherlands now has a majority of private schools which are run by independent boards.

The unique characteristics of the Dutch education system have often been used as a reference point for both positive and negative arguments about choice elsewhere in the world, "often with little factual basis" as Glenn (1989) pointed out. The problem with using the Dutch model in this way is that often little or no attention is paid to the specific socio-cultural setting that keeps the country's unique education policies in place (Walford, 1995). Even more important, it neglects the question as to whether the solution arrived at in the Dutch situation of 1917 is still appropriate in a contemporary context. In this article, we will describe the relations which have developed historically, the way the system of free school choice actually operates as well as some contemporary issues.

Historical Growth of the System of Free Choice

To gain a full understanding of the exceptional character of the Dutch system it is necessary to go back to its historical roots. These can be traced back to the beginning of the 19th century when, under the influence of the French Revolution, the first steps toward the establishment of a modern nation were taken. The equality of all citizens was officially recognised for the first time and the Dutch Reformed Church lost its status as the Established Church. Catholics were able to practise their faith openly and became eligible for public office from that time. This enabled the Catholics, who constituted about 35 per cent of the Dutch population, to achieve greater emancipation for themselves.

The next step toward further liberalisation and modernisation was taken in 1848, once again under the influence of revolutionary developments abroad. That was the year in which the government relinquished the state monopoly over education and freedom of education was laid down in the Constitution. This gave the supporters of independent schools the freedom to found the so-called 'free schools', to finance them from their own resources and organise them in accordance with their own convictions. Orthodox Protestants were the most keen to take this opportunity because they were not satisfied with the Christian teaching given in the state schools. Originating as a movement within the church, this group of Protestants developed into a political party whose main slogan was 'for free schools'. This led to the beginning of the so-called 'schools struggle' in the Netherlands.

The struggle in itself was not exceptional, because all over Europe in the 18th and 19th centuries a conflict was being played out between church and state. It arose because of the interest which an enlightened citizenry started, around the end of the 18th century, to attach to national systems of mass education to build modern nation states. Elements in this were: the declaration that education was a matter of national interest, the introduction of legislation to make education compulsory, the establishment of national ministries for education and the setting-up of national schools inspectorates (Ramirez & Boli, 1987). The expansion of this 'continental model', developed by the great powers of the time (France and Prussia), went hand in hand with resistance on the part of the church which had been responsible for education up till then and in many cases was also an 'established church'. Until that time there had been what Archer (1979) termed 'mono-integration', that is to say education was monopolised by a religious elite. This meant that other institutions, such as the state, armed forces and the market, did not benefit directly from education.

Archer has shown that hardly anywhere in Europe did the state succeed in breaking the monopoly of the church. Where liberal élites tried to provide education through local communities or on a market basis, religious organisations managed to regain power over the schools through those communities or via the market. In the Netherlands, as in many other countries, the struggle went through various phases. In the first phase the dispute centred around the ideological nature of education. The second phase was about winning freedom of education, and in the third phase the struggle concentrated on the obtaining of state subsidies for denominational or private schools.

What was unique about the Dutch situation was that this struggle, which went on from the middle of the 19th century to the Pacification in 1917, coincided with the beginning of a general social transformation which is known as the process of 'compartmentalisation' or 'pillarisation' (in Dutch 'verzuiling'). This process institutionalised a peculiar form of 'pluralism', that is a strong vertical segmentation of all sectors of social life along (religious) ideological dividing lines. Each religious or quasi-religious group created its own social world, covering the entire life-span of an individual from nursery school, via sports club, trade union, university, hospital, broadcasting corporation to burial society. The phenomenon can be said to have dominated Dutch society from 1870 to 1960.

'Compartmentalisation' not only brought people together in highly segregated socio-cultural settings and organisations, it also provided an important structure through which government tasks were increasingly executed. One of the clearest examples of both these aspects of 'compartmentalisation' is provided by the school system. Initially, private education was provided by religious entrepreneurs for each religious group, but when financing was taken over by the state, religious-based organisations continued to provide the service and started acting as quasi-governmental bodies. In the 1960s the golden age of 'compartmentalisation' came to an end and a process of deinstitutionalisation or 'decompartmentalisation' slowly began.

The process of 'compartmentalisation' in education can be clearly traced in the growth in the market share of private education. Figure 1 shows how much the market share of private (mainly denominational) education has grown since the middle of the nineteenth century. Freedom of education established in the 1848 Constitution gave private education a free rein to capture an important market share. Around 1880 about a quarter of pupils were attending private schools. This is a remarkably high number because, although private schools had been legally allowed before that time, they had not received any government subsidy. Evidently the schools dispute had managed to mobilise sufficient support that parents and church bodies were willing to donate sufficient funds to found and run their 'own schools'.

The more pronounced growth in the period from 1890 to 1910 is easy to explain. In 1888 the Catholics, who until then had supported the Liberals and their legislation, entered into a coalition government with the Protestants. This coalition, which later would expand into a robust power block, was striving to gain further subsidies for private education. Partial subsidy was granted in 1889, even though it had to be won at local level. The increase in the level of subsidy in 1905, and the Compulsory Education Act of 1901, largely account for the further increase in the market share between 1900 and 1910.

Of course, the great leap forward came after the Pacification. In the period after 1920 the proportion of public to private schools underwent a radical reversal: Dutch education changed from being a predominantly public system to a predominantly private system. Private education gained a market share of around 70 per cent, rising to 73 per cent in the first decades after the Second World War. After that the percentage continued to hover around 68 per cent (33 per cent Catholic, 30 per cent Protestant and 5 per cent non-denominational private). The radical turnaround after 1920 can be explained: it is due to the private schools being given complete equal treatment with the state schools. The fact that the market share remained constant after 1960 is not so easy to account for.

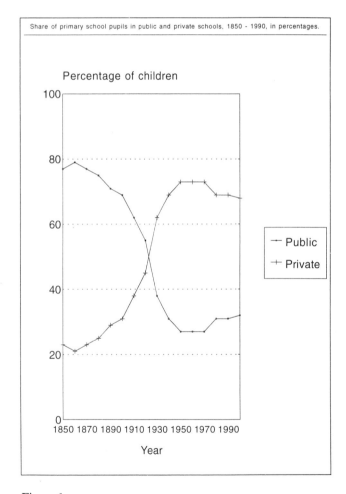

Share of primary school pupils in public and private schools, 1850 - 1990, in percentages.

Figure 1.

Developments in the period after 1970 certainly require further explanation. First, this period was characterised by a sharp fall in the birth rate. This fall led to increased competition between schools for pupils. Second, although this was a period characterised by secularisation and decompartmentalisation, this is hardly reflected in the figures at all. Only the Catholic sector lost a small proportion of its pupils between 1970 and 1990. The Protestant and public sectors remained constant, while the proportion in non-denominational private schools increased.

Three different explanations have been offered for this rather puzzling continuation of compartmentalisation in education (Dronkers, 1992). The first explanation seeks its cause in the motivations behind parental choice. It appears that parents who do not go to church still feel the need to give their children some religious standards and values and so they exhibit a preference for private schools. Many arguments have been put forward against this explanation. Research into the reasons behind school choice, which we will discuss in greater length in the next section, shows that religious motives no longer play a major part in the choice of denominational schools. Moreover, these studies have also shown that many denominational schools no longer provide genuine religious socialisation.

The second explanation is based more on institutional grounds. It is based on the assumption that legislation and political forces operate to the advantage of private education. According to this explanation, the religious parties are in a position of power which gives them a firm grasp on educational provision and so limits the range of choice available to parents. Although there are indications that there are definitely some grounds for this explanation, it is certainly not the whole story. No explanation has been found as to why non-religious parents do not use their right to a free choice of school to turn their backs on the denominational schools ('voting with their feet'). There must be some reason why they (still) feel at home in the denominational schools.

The third reason tries to meet the objections to the second explanation, again looking for the main cause in the reasons for the parents' choice. It is said that the reason why non-religious parents decide to send their children to religious schools is because, on average, those schools are more effective. A difference between the effectiveness of the average public and the average denominational school has been demonstrated time and again by research (for example, Laarhoven et al, 1986; Laarhoven et al, 1990), and parents notice this whether directly or not. If this explanation is correct, it could mean that the traditional divisions along religious dividing lines have been replaced by a new dividing mechanism, namely that of the (quasi-)market where competition is based on the success of the schools.

The Actual Functioning of the Educational Market

If we consider an education system as a (quasi-)market mechanism, we should first explain what a (quasi-)market actually is. A market has a supply side and a demand side. In education the supply side consists of the providers of education, in other words the schools. The demand side comprises the parents and students who are the consumers of education. This market is only a quasi-market because, although the suppliers are encouraged to compete against each other and consumers are encouraged to express their preferences, no money actually changes hands (Bartlett, 1992). Woods (1994) states that, in a market, producers are supposed to respond to consumer choice. The rationale behind educational reforms which stimulate parental choice is that *"choice will change schools"* (Woods, 1994, p. 124). It is claimed that choice will improve the way schools operate and the service they give. We can only expect to get any educational benefit from school choice if parents can make an informed choice and if there is a degree of diversity between schools (Stillman & Maychell, 1986).

Before looking into the situation in the Netherlands, we would like to make a few critical observations on the idea of the market functioning in education. First, the consumption of education is not a matter of free choice but a legal obligation. Second, education is a complicated product and it is very difficult to make an objective comparison between schools. Third, education is, by its very nature, very personal, depending a great deal on human concerns. Choosing a school is very different from going to a supermarket. Fourth, schools are not always able to respond to the demand for their education. A popular school cannot expand endlessly without losing its attractiveness, and when schools have to turn students away the market mechanism is disturbed.

It is on the demand side that a lot of research has been carried out. A large number of studies into the motives behind school choice have been conducted in the Netherlands, far more than in Britain and the other European countries. This is accounted for by the freedom of school choice, the great diversity between schools and recent changes in the motivation behind parental choice of schools which makes it an interesting subject for investigation. Three different traditions can be distinguished in the research in this field (Van der Wouw, 1994). Versloot (1990) gives a detailed overview. The first type of research has investigated parental views on various characteristics of schools and the relationships between these characteristics and the parents' backgrounds. Studies of this kind have been conducted since 1968. A second type of research, which has mainly been concentrated in primary education, has concerned itself with (ethnic) segregation. Research in this area has received increasing political attention since 1986, since it seems that the school choices made by white Dutch parents could be causing increasing ethnic segregation between schools. Indeed, Van der Wouw

(1994) concludes that the ethnic composition of a school appears to be an independent motive for school choice itself. A third type of research has been contextual research. This means research in the context of a certain group of schools. It is in this field of research that we find the three-motives model of quality, distance and denomination which was introduced in 1983 (Pelkmans et al). Quite a number of studies in this field (Boef-van der Meulen et al, 1983; Pelkmans et al,1983; Pieters, 1992; Versloot, 1993; De Vries, 1987) found that parents choose a school primarily on the basis of quality, while accessibility (distance) and denomination come in second and third place (Witziers & De Groot, 1993). As a general rule therefore, parents opt for a good school, rather than a neighbourhood school or a school of a particular denomination. Although these three characteristics are not mutually exclusive, parental choice of schools tends to be a deliberate one based on what they think is the best school. This is something which is very difficult for them to verify. The quality of a school is very difficult (if not impossible) to determine compared to its location or denomination.

This trend toward choosing schools for more deliberate but less verifiable reasons, has increased the scope for schools to stress their distinctive features. This brings us to the supply side of our market mechanism. Very little empirical research has been conducted in the Netherlands on the functioning of schools within the market mechanism. With their increased autonomy and the introduction of block-grant funding, schools have become more dependent on a stable student intake. From case studies of three secondary schools in Rotterdam, we know that schools are increasingly stressing their distinctive features (Teelken, 1995). They are concerned to attract a certain number of students, but they also want an academically balanced intake. Striving for a balanced intake meant that all three of the schools studied made special efforts to attract academically able students.

Because schools cannot be certain about their student numbers, one can expect competition between schools. From economic theory one would expect competition between suppliers to have a beneficial effect. De Jong (1985) mentions two functions of competition, an allocation and an innovative function. The allocation function refers to the process of choice: because resources are limited, consumers have to choose an optimal combination of supplies. When schools experience competition they are more likely to use their scarce resources carefully and try to let students benefit from them directly. The innovative function is apparent when organisations are more willing to take risks or introduce new products. When schools are subject to competition they are more willing to offer new and more differentiated forms of education. This gives students the opportunity to select the most suitable school. The empirical findings of Roeleveld & Dronkers (1994) suggest that schools of different denominations are most effective when their sector supplies a reasonable share (about 40 per cent) of the student market, without any specific denomination having a definite majority. In this situation one can expect a degree of competition between schools. One assumes that competing schools will try to achieve the best possible outcomes for the largest number of students. If that is the case, it is possible that competition would improve educational results. This again implies that the market mechanism has a beneficial effect on education.

In Britain, Walford (1990) argued, the 1988 Education Reform Act reintroduced the market into education with the consequent ending of egalitarianism and reinforcement of the existing social order. This has not happened in the Netherlands where, at least in a formal sense, a market mechanism has always been present (freedom of supply and demand since 1917). First, there is great diversity between schools, mainly religious diversity. Second, although selection in secondary education is quite strict (four streams) it is based purely on academic criteria. There are no fee-paying schools. Educational choice can only have a beneficial effect on schools if parents are able to make a deliberate choice between equally good schools which offer a certain diversity in curriculum, atmosphere, pedagogical orientation and so on.

The diversity of schools in the Netherlands is upheld by the constitutional right to freedom in matters of education. However, this freedom has recently been affected by a number of factors. Decreasing student numbers and large numbers of mergers, as well as the impossibility of creating new sources of supply in education, raise questions as to whether the threefold freedom of education still exists. A recent publication on freedom of education in the primary and secondary sectors (Meijer et al, 1995) distinguished four domains in which freedom can be exercised: at the organisational level, in the admission and exclusion of students, the recruitment of staff and human resource management and administrative set-up. Freedom of organisation is still used by schools. Both primary and secondary schools stress their distinctive identity, which consists not only of their denomination but also their educational visions and alignment to a particular pupil composition. Regarding student admissions, private schools rarely use their right to refuse students on the grounds of conviction. The schools only ask the students to respect their religion and educational ideology. The same is required of staff, although schools with a certain educational profile sometimes have rather stricter qualification requirements. Regarding administrative set-up, the general influence of different groups of stakeholders varies between schools which allows for different administrative set-ups. So the freedom to organise education and to design one's own administrative set-up does still exist. With regard to the other two domains, if schools do not use their constitutional freedoms this is their own choice. It is possible therefore to conclude that freedom of education does still exist.

Recent Developments and Problems

Traditional ideological diversity has determined the composition and organisation of the Dutch education system to an important extent. This is mainly expressed in the great diversity of schools founded on ideological convictions. In addition, just as in all other western industrial countries, social class has left its mark on the system. Up to now this has mainly been expressed in the clearly distinguished and selective types of secondary education, but not in denominational distinctions. With the exception of non-denominational private education, the different denominations have always provided a service for pupils from all social classes. According to some (Dronkers, 1995), this is one of the main reasons why élite schools have not developed in the Netherlands.

After the Second World War urbanisation and migration profoundly changed Dutch society. Regional differences became less important and what remained was differences between inner cities, suburbs and the countryside and differences between districts within the large cities. New lifestyles emerged as a result of increased welfare and geographic mobility, a rise in the general level of education in the population and the increasing importance of the mass media. These changes undermined the traditional social 'compartments' in the 1960s and 1970s and they began to lose their grip on social life. Secularisation and individualisation became the key ideas. In addition, immigrants from the former colonies, migrant workers and refugees brought new cultures and religions with them. This changed the nature of ideological diversity in Dutch society. In broad outline there were three distinct developments:

- change in the position of different ideologies and the institutionalisation of that change in separate organisations (key word: secularisation);
- new trends and lifestyles (key word: individualisation);
- influx of new ideologies and cultural identities (key word: ethnicity).

What is the significance of these developments for supply and demand on the education market and in what way is recent government policy responding to these developments?

The *first* development is evident in the marked rise of secularisation: the number of people who do not belong to any religious group has grown from only a few percent in the last century to almost 60 per cent of the population (one of the highest percentages in Europe). It is expected that this group will expand even more to become almost three-quarters of the population by 2020. Alongside the decreasing role of religion one can point to the greatly reduced importance of religious and ideological differentiation as the framework on which social life is organised. This is clearly visible in the fall in the number of marriages between people with the same religion, for example, and the disappearance of organisations based on a religious foundation.

In religious circles this development has mainly led to a *redefinition* and *regrouping* of denominational interests. Redefinition here means a liberalisation of the religious character of the organisations in social life. Bureaucratic professionalisation has gradually replaced ideological commitment as the most important identifying feature of these organisations. Values and objectives other than those which are exclusively Christian are in use. Catholic education, in particular, has broadened its identity (Meijer et al, 1995). Not only are children from other faiths welcomed into Catholic schools, the religious criteria for staff and the curriculum are also less strict.

Regrouping mainly takes the form of interdenominational links: Catholics and the various Protestant denominations combine to form a single association, often letting go of their specific denominational background. The best-known example is the formation of a single religious political party, the Christian Democrat Party, which now projects itself more as a party of the centre than as a religious party. In education, the interfaith or interdenominational school has made its appearance, but it cannot be said to have had a spectacular growth. At the moment only 50 out of around 8,000 primary schools are interdenominational, though this may increase in the future as a result of mergers.

For a long time the government was rather unresponsive to this development. As late as 1991, when international examiners from the OECD raised a question about the freedom of education in their report on the Netherlands because of its possible negative impact on equity and its high cost, policy-makers replied that the Dutch population did not want a change. However, within the framework of a scaling-up operation in primary education, the Secretary of State for Education set up a committee of experts in 1994 to advise on "bringing the body of schools into line with developments in society as far as possible". In accordance with the Dutch tradition this committee came forward with a compromise solution proposing a moderate change: the so-called 'coexistence' schools and school boards. A 'coexistence' school would have to be administered by a general school board under which schools of different faiths (for example a Catholic and a Muslim school) would work together. This proposal was not adopted by the government, but it illustrates the fact that changes are still being sought within the framework of the existing system.

The *second* development can be summed up as the rise of individualism, that is the growing need of individuals to shape their own lives. Several (foreign) authors (including Kennedy, 1995) have observed that this cultural change has taken place very quickly in the Netherlands and has been relatively all-embracing. Since the 1960s the Netherlands has changed within a short period of time from a traditional religious country to a society where anything *seems* to be possible (abortion on demand, drugs, euthanasia and so on). In comparison with other countries the Netherlands scores relatively highly on views about individual liberty and individualism (Halman et al, 1987; Hofstede, 1980).

A noticeable difference compared with countries like the United States and England, which also score highly on individualism, is that the 'reactionary' impulse in the 1980s which came as a response to the cultural changes of the 60s and 70s has been quite weak. There is no 'moral majority' fighting back for the moral values of the past such as there was under Reagan and Thatcher (the 'New Right'). Nevertheless the neo-liberal ideal of less government and leaving more to market forces has taken root in Dutch politics. This notion is certainly present in the field of education, even if it is not very popular among the educational élite (Karsten et al, 1995). There is a general trend toward deregulation and increased autonomy which includes the extension market forces.

Various methods have been considered to increase market forces in the supply and demand of schools. First, there is a discussion in progress about the introduction of vouchers. Although in the Netherlands a substantial proportion of funding already goes via the consumer, in vocational and higher education ideas are being exchanged about having an even stricter relationship between registration and funding. However, nothing has got beyond the planning stage in this area.

Second, consideration is being given to how to improve the information given to parents. A meeting between the government and the national representatives of the school boards agreed to make it a legal requirement that each school should produce a school brochure for parents and pupils. This document, for which a model has been developed, must help parents and pupils to make reasoned choices of schools.

Third, in the primary school sector an opportunity has been created to use parental surveys to assess the potential interest in different kinds of schools directly. A decision to found a new school could then be based on the results of the surveys. Naturally this method can only be used where new schools are to be built (new housing estates and rapidly expanding conurbations).

Finally, there has been a proposal to reduce restrictions on the foundation of new schools by granting more generous part-funding and temporary funding of schools. However, this plan is not yet in operation.

To summarise, one can say that in response to the rising demand for greater individual freedom of choice, plans to extend the influence of market forces have only been carried out in a piecemeal fashion. This means that the majority of parents still have to choose the school that is best for them from within the existing provision. Given that since the 1970s parental choice of schools has been less firmly based on religious grounds, it appears that a 'quiet revolution' has been taking place. Behind the facade of public and denominational schools hide recent differences in effectiveness: measured in terms of pupils' results denominational schools do better generally than public schools. As a result of this, disparities in parental awareness of the relative effectiveness of different schools, which itself correlates with their own level of education, can perhaps be seen as the basis for a new form of inequality (Dronkers, 1995).

The *third* development manifests itself through the increasing importance of immigrants in the population. For almost thirty years the Netherlands has had greater levels of immigration than emigration. The large influx of immigrants between 1960 and the present day have mainly originated from the Mediterranean and the former Dutch colony of Surinam (Karsten & Leeman, 1988). The former group has been dominated by Turks and Moroccans. This change in the make-up of the population, the most important consequence of which has been an increase in cultural and religious pluralism, has been dealt with up to now in primary education by internal differentiation (increased cultural differentiation within existing schools) and external differentiation (founding of 'own' schools).

The increase in cultural differentiation among existing schools has been an uneven development. Not all schools over the whole country exhibit the same degree of differentiation. There is an uneven distribution of children from ethnic minorities in the different parts of the country, in different districts within the larger cities and also among schools of different denominations. By far the majority of schools with over half of their pupils from ethnic minorities are found in the four major cities in the west of the country: Amsterdam, Rotterdam, Den Haag and Utrecht. Within these cities the distribution is uneven between different districts. However, what is remarkable is that not all the schools within the same district have the same concentration of ethnic minorities. This indicates that some schools are (able to be) more selective in their admissions. In general one finds the lowest proportion of pupils from ethnic minorities in non-denominational private schools and the highest in public schools. The range is wide for all types of school, however, with examples of both extreme under-representation and extreme over-representation of pupils from ethnic minorities in many schools.

A study by Dors et al (1991) which covered 23 per cent of all primary school pupils in the Netherlands found that about a third of primary schools could be classified as 'concentration schools'. This study also showed that there is a relationship between ethnicity and social background, although the pupils from ethnic minorities are more unevenly distributed than pupils from lower social backgrounds. This indicates that following the earlier 'class flights', private education (especially non-religious) has become a 'safe haven' for white pupils. This puts policy-makers on the horns of a political dilemma: there is a conflict between a commitment to freedom of choice on the one hand and an even stronger commitment to equal opportunities on the other hand. Finally, the same study also demonstrated that neither the local authorities nor the school boards see any possibility, within existing legislation, of regulating pupil admissions to achieve a more balanced distribution. One of the study's policy recommendations to come to some kind of controlled choice was immediately rejected by the Ministry of

Education because it would imply a fundamental change to long-standing education legislation.

External differentiation got off to a slow start in the late 1980s. Muslim and Hindu groups started to found their 'own' schools on a very limited scale. At the present time there are 29 primary schools being run on Islamic principles and three primary schools on Hindu principles. Research into the reasons behind parental choice of schools in Amsterdam (Breenen et al, 1991) showed that the demand for Muslim schools is probably greater than the supply. Turkish parents express the strongest support with 70 per cent being in favour of schools being founded on Islamic principles. Moroccan parents are rather more cautious, but still 86 per cent are either in favour or have no objection and only 5 per cent are against. Among Turkish parents 12 per cent are against. Another study (Shadid & Van Koningsveld, 1992) showed that these schools are trying to achieve a twofold goal: strengthening of the community's own (religious) identity and improvement of the quality of education. In the case of the Islamic schools the importance of religion is evident from the fact that those who took the initial steps to found the schools came mainly from traditional religious circles. Some doubts have been expressed about this, however. The doubters argue that the founding of Islamic schools is an ideological-political matter rather than a religious matter (Kabdan, 1992 among others).

The response to the founding of (mainly Islamic) 'own' schools has been mixed. Fairly positive reactions have been heard coming from religious groups as they recall their own past emancipation. In the local authorities where the requests are submitted the reaction is usually one of firm rejection. They fear that separate schools lead to further isolation of minorities within Dutch society. The national government usually adopts a fairly formal attitude: there is essentially no reason to treat the foundation of these schools any differently from those of other religious groups.

Conclusions

This article has demonstrated how the present Dutch education system has evolved out of a struggle for religious and political freedom. This struggle led to the current broad diversity of schools, with parents and students having the freedom to choose any school they wanted. Of course, this choice is not necessarily granted. Private schools do not have to grant each family the right to attend just because they are the school of choice, and oversubscribed private schools sometimes have long waiting lists. Such schools can develop their own criteria for selection (some open, some hidden). However, private schools are not allowed to discriminate on criteria irrelevant to the denomination such as ethnic background or gender. Such discrimination is hard to prove and, in practice, some schools refuse certain groups of children. On the other hand, few public schools have 'waiting lists'. Each local authority has to provide enough places in public schools, but the choice for a specific public school does not have to be granted. However, until recently, the extent of diversity has prevented the development of any sharp social differences between schools.

Three major developments have had an influence upon the Dutch education system since the 1960s: secularisation, individualism and immigration. Strong secularisation has led to new proposals on how schools should be governed, but all of these either remain within the existing system or have not been implemented.

Individualisation has led to the incorporation of more elements of the market in education, as changing motives for parental choice of schools and increased autonomy of schools has given the schools more scope to stress their distinctive features and to make their own policies. However, although various proposals have been made to strengthen the market mechanism in education, none of them have been introduced except for the school brochures.

Immigration has increased ethnic diversity between school populations, mainly due to over and under-representation of ethnic minorities in the schools in the larger cities.

Despite these developments the Dutch education system can still be regarded as a very diverse but essentially egalitarian system. Up to now the increased influence of market forces has not changed that substantially.

References

Archer, M. (1979) *The Social Origins of Educational Systems.* London: Sage.

Bartlett, Will (1992) *Studies in Decentralisation and Quasi-markets, Quasi-markets and Educational Reforms: a case study.* Bristol: University of Bristol.

Boef-van der Meulen, S., Bronneman-Helmers, R., Konings-van der Snoek, M. (1983) *Schoolkeuzemotieven en meningen over onderwijs.* Rijswijk: Sociaal en Cultureel Planbureau.

Breenen, K. van, Jong, U. de, Klerk, L. de, Berdowski, Z. & Steenhoven, P. van der (1991) *Etnische scheidslijnen in het Amsterdamse basisonderwijs, een keuze?* Amsterdam: Gemeente Amsterdam.

Dors, H.G., Karsten, S., Ledoux, G. & Steen, A.H.M. (1991) *Etnische segregatie in het onderwijs: beleidsaspecten.* Amsterdam: SCO.

Dronkers, J. (1992) Blijvende onderwijsverzuiling ondanks secularisering: een onbedoeld effect van overheidsbeleid? *Mens en Maatschappij,* 5, pp. 227-237.

Dronkers, J. (1995) The Existence of Parental Choice in the Netherlands, *Educational Policy,* 9, pp. 227-243.

Glenn, C.L. (1989) *Choice of Schools in Six Nations.* Washington: U.S. Government Printing Office.

Halman, L. et al *(1987) Traditie, secularisatie en individualisering.* Tilburg: Tilburg University Press.

Hofstede, G. (1980) *Culture's Consequences: international differences in work-related values.* Beverley Hills: Sage.

James, E. (1984) Benefits and costs of privatized public services: lessons from the Dutch educational system, *Comparative Education Review,* 28, pp. 605-624.

Jong, H.W. de (1985) *Dynamische Markttheorie.* Leiden: Stenfert Kroese.

Kabdan, R. (1992) Op weg naar maatschappelijke spanningen op religieuze gronden, islamitische scholen in Nederland zijn onwenselijk, *Vernieuwing,* 51(9), pp. 4-8.

Karsten, S & Leeman, Y. (1988) Holland in Surinam, Surinamese in Holland, *Compare,* 18, pp. 63-77.

Karsten, S., Groot, I. & Ruiz, M.A. (1995) Value orientations of the Dutch educational élite, *Comparative Education Review,* 39, pp. 508-523.

Kennedy, J. (1995) *Nieuw Babylon in Aanbouw: Nederland in de jaren zestig.* Amsterdam/Meppel: Boom.

Kwaasteniet, M. de (1990) *Denomination and Primary Education in the Netherlands (1870-1984).* Amsterdam: Koninklijk Nederlands Aardrijkskundig Genootschap.

Louis, K.S., Bodstrom, L. & Teichler, U. (1990) *Review of Educational Policies: the Netherlands.* Paris: OECD.

Meijer, J., Peetsma, T.T.D., Vermeulen, M., Karsten, S. (1995) *Vrijheid van inrichting, onderzoek onder bestuur en schoolleiding.* Amsterdam: SCO-Kohnstamm Instituut.

Meijer, J. et al (1996) *Vrijheid van Inrichting.* De Lier: ABC.

Pelkmans, A.H.W.M. et al (1983) *Wensen omtrent scholen en de onderwijsplanning; vijf deelonderzoekingen over kwalitatieve onderwijsbehoeften, 'verlangd onderwijs' en de planning van het voortgezet onderwijs.* Nijmegen: ITS.

Pieters, L. (1992) Trends in schoolkeuze na de basisschool, *Meso,* 64, pp. 25-30.

Ramirez, F.O. & Boli, J. (1987) The political construction of mass schooling: European origins and worldwide institutionalization, *Sociology of Education,* 60, pp. 2-17.

Roeleveld, Jaap & Dronkers, Jaap (1994) Bijzondere scholen of buitengewone scholen? *Mens en Maatschappij,* 69(1), pp. 85-108.

Shadid, W.A. & Koningsveld, P.S. van (1992) Islamitische scholen. De verschillende scholen en hun achtergronden, *Samenwijs,* pp. 227-233.

Stillman, Andy & Maychell, Karen (1986) *Choosing Schools: Parents, LEAs and the 1980 Education Act.* Windsor: NFER-Nelson.

Teelken, J.C. (1995) Verzelfstandiging en identiteit van scholen voor voortgezet onderwijs, een casestudie in Rotterdam, in ORD-bundel *Onderwijsonderzoek in Nederland en Vlaanderen.* Groningen: GION.

Versloot, A.M. (1990) *Ouders en vrijheid van onderwijs: schoolkeuze in de provincie Utrecht.* De Lier: ABC (dissertation).

Vries, A. de (1987) Kiezen voor een school. Schoolkeuze en marketing: een analyse van de 'afnemers' in het onderwijs. *Meso,* March 1987, pp. 22-26.

Walford, G. (1990) Developing choice in British education, *Compare,* 20, pp. 67-81.

Walford, G (1995) Faith-based grant-maintained schools: selective international borrowing from the Netherlands, *Journal of Educational Policy,* 10, pp. 245-257.

Witziers, B. & Groot, I.N. de (1993) *Concurrentie tussen scholen, Een onderzoek naar de marketingmiddelen die scholen inzetten om hun concurrentiepositie te verbeteren en de wettelijke context waarbinnen scholen concurreren.* Enschede: OCTO.

Woods, Philip (1994) School responses to the quasi-market, in J. Mark Halstead (Ed.) *Parental Choice and Education.* London: Kogan Page.

Wouw, B.A.J. van der (1994) *Schoolkeuze tussen wensen en realisering, een onderzoek naar verklaring voor veranderingen in schoolkeuzepatronen vanuit het perspectief van (etnische) segregatie.* Middelburg: OOMO series, Tandem Felix.

Oxford Studies in Comparative Education, Vol. 6(1), 1996

Choice and the Quasi-market in Swedish Education

GARY MIRON

Over the past five years a number of rapid and sweeping reforms have brought about a restructuring of the Swedish education system. These reforms – characterized by decentralisation, privatisation and the increasing emphasis on market forces, choice and competition – have affected all levels of the education system. The speed with which they were planned, approved and implemented permitted no time for piloting. In fact, there was no time for involving any other than the politicians who debated the reform.

These neo-liberal reforms constitute an anachronism in the traditionally centrally-steered and egalitarian Sweden. Sweden is renowned for its emphasis on political consensus and the broad involvement of researchers and practitioners in the planning of education reforms. These reforms are typically piloted beforehand and carefully monitored during implementation. The comprehensive school reform which ended the parallel school system is often used as a good example of how to conduct an education reform. In fact, Sweden has provided a number of "textbook examples" of how to plan, test and implement education reforms. Seen against this background, and in light of the neo-liberal reforms that have recently taken place, one can only wonder if the Swedish reforms of the 1990s will come to serve as examples of how not to conduct education reforms.

Recent Reforms Concerning Restructuring

While 1992 marked the year of the so-called "free choice revolution" in Sweden, one can see indications of the ensuing reforms long before. During the 1980s, the municipal schools were granted more and more flexibility to create their own profiles, and further steps were taken to allow schools to operate outside the municipal school system (Marklund, 1986). Deregulation and decentralisation were important themes during the late 1980s. The municipal governments were given more and more of the responsibility for planning and administering social services, including education. Likewise, the municipalities received more responsibility for financial matters and decision-making in matters concerning the distribution of resources. In 1989, central regulations concerning the positions and salaries of school employees were abolished, and in 1991 the municipalities received the state's share of funding for formal schooling in one lump sum, rather than several smaller sums earmarked for each level or type of schooling.

In 1991, Parliament approved legislation (Government Bill 1990/1991:115) requiring the municipalities to distribute resources to both public and independent schools in the same way as was done for municipal schools (i.e. based upon the specific needs of each school). Approved independent schools would be given public money for the instruction they provided.

After the national election in 1991, the Social Democratic-led government was replaced by a coalition of four centre/right political parties. The new government declared a "free-choice revolution". Improved conditions for private alternatives and the right to choose were emphasised in several social services, including all levels of the education system. By March 1992, a new proposition was prepared (Government Bill 1991/92:95) concerning the introduction of school vouchers for approved compulsory-level independent schools. This was approved in June 1992 and went into effect the following month, thus superseding the legislation approved in 1991. The new reform required municipalities to distribute at least 85 per cent of the average per-student cost in the municipal schools for each student enrolled in approved independent schools. The 15 per cent reduction of average per-student costs was justified by the fact that independent schools were not required to provide school heath care, home language training, free meals and transportation, etc. At the same time, the municipalities were obliged to provide places for all students within their borders regardless of ability and distance to school.

The amount of public financing and the working conditions for the independent schools were viewed by many as being among the most favourable conditions in the world for private schools. During the first two years of this reform essentially all applications to establish new independent schools were approved. Additionally, there was little supervision of the independent schools – at least initially. The responsibility for supervising these schools was given to the newly established National Agency for Education, and the municipal authorities had no legal right to supervise these schools nor to assess how the money was being used, even though they were forced to fund them. The independent schools were still allowed to charge fees, but the legislation stated that these fees were to be "reasonable". Compared to similar reforms in other countries, there were very few restrictions or safeguards.

In 1993, similar reforms were made in upper-secondary schools and in schools for children with mental retardation. Reforms in the administration and financing of higher education were also introduced which gave the universities and other higher education bodies more autonomy and linked parts of their funding to output indicators. Two public universities were put under non-state ownership (i.e. converted into foundations). In fact, since the pre-school services were already allowing choice and using child care vouchers in a great many municipalities, one can say that the entire formal education system of Sweden has been touched by the reforms dealing with decentralisation, choice and the use of market forces.

In addition to the school voucher scheme, the Conservative government also managed to introduce a new grading system and a new national curriculum during their three years in power. The new national curriculum, which was approved in 1994, provided students with more chances than earlier to choose which subjects they wished to participate in or to study indepth. Likewise, schools acquired more freedom and greater choice in deciding how to attain the specified goals for each subject in the national curriculum, as well as how to distribute the number of hours of instruction per subject. Municipal schools were granted the freedom and encouraged to create their own "profile" within a specific subject area or according to a particular theme. The new curriculum placed more emphasis on centrally-defined goals, which marked a shift in the role of the central government from planning the inputs to evaluating outputs. Consequently, most of the administration, planning and the responsibility for resource distribution for compulsory and upper secondary schooling has been decentralised and left to the municipalities or to the schools themselves.

In 1994, the Social Democrats won sufficient support in the national elections to regain control of the government. During the election campaign, one of the Social Democrats' campaign promises was to remove school vouchers and to return to the arrangements established in the 1991 reform proposal. After the election, however, the Social Democrats have hesitated in removing the voucher system, although in 1995 they reduced the size of the school voucher from 85 per cent to 75 per cent of the average municipal per-student cost. A Commission was also appointed to examine the current voucher system and the regulations surrounding independent schools. Among the issues taken up by the Commission were those dealing with how to increase the role and influence of municipalities in the approval and supervision of independent schools. Based upon the recommendations of the Commission, the government presented a new proposal in May 1996. This will be voted on in the autumn of 1996. If approved, a large number of changes will be made in the manner in which independent schools are financed and supervised. The main points in the new proposal are included below:

(i) school vouchers will disappear and the independent schools will receive money from the municipalities based upon their needs;
(ii) an independent school can be denied financing if this causes substantial and tangible negative consequences for the municipality in question;

(iii) student fees will be forbidden for independent schools receiving public financing;

(iv) a minimum of 20 students will be required in order for an independent school to be approved;

(v) demands for approval will increase and independent schools will be obliged to more closely follow the general goals and values spelled out in the national curriculum; and

(vi) independent schools will be required to provide school heath care services and home language instruction for children of immigrant background.

The Social Democrats had hoped to gain support for their new proposition from at least one of the centre or right-wing parties. Thus far, this has not happened, and so they will have to rely upon the Green Party or the Left Party in order to approve this. The Social Democratic government claims that these changes will provide "equivalent" conditions for independent and municipal schools since both will receive funding based upon their needs. A few of the parties, who are now in opposition, claim that this reform will lead to a slow strangulation of the independent schools. They vow, therefore, to tear up this reform if and when they return to power. The long-standing importance of consensus on education issues seems widely disregarded now, and the likelihood that any government can develop a education reform that can survive a political election is greatly reduced.

Theoretically, choice has always been possible in Sweden; yet, the long-standing practice is that all children are assigned to a school based upon proximity. While much of the attention has been on the centrally-legislated school voucher scheme for independent schools, a number of urban municipalities have also introduced competition among their schools, with school voucher-like incentives. Some of them did this even before the 1992 reform for independent schools. In the municipalities with open enrolment, nearly 80 per cent of all students choosing a school other than the one they were assigned are actually attending another municipal school rather than a private alternative. Currently, the law concerning school choice among public schools states that the wishes of parents and students concerning school placement should be followed to the greatest extent possible. However, the principle of choice does not go before the principle of proximity (i.e., a given school should provide places for all the students in its catchment area before providing places for others). Furthermore, a municipality does not need to satisfy a request for a student to attend another school, if it creates economic or organisational problems. Pressing social reasons, however, could quickly lead to placement in another school.

Forces Behind the Reform

The issue of school choice and the use of market forces in schools has arisen in many countries in recent years. A number of factors can be related to the introduction of school reforms concerning decentralisation, privatisation, choice and the use of market forces. Based upon a review of literature in a number of countries, Daun & Miron (1994) have distinguished and discussed five such factors: (i) economic decline; (ii) decreasing legitimacy of the state; (iii) cultural revitalisation; (iv) declining levels of educational achievement; and (v) purely ideological and political factors.

The reforms in Sweden seem to be particularly motivated by economic factors. The prevalent economic trend from the 1940s to the 1970s was toward increasingly greater equality and wellbeing, paid for with increasingly greater taxes. The deepening economic crisis in the 1980s stopped this trend. By the onset of the 1990s, Sweden had joined a host of other OECD countries that were faced with high unemployment, large national debts and slow economic growth. The poor state of the economy has led to demands for more efficiency in all the social sectors. At the same time, increased economic competition has led to more emphasis on improving the quality of schooling in order to make the work force more competitive.

Political factors have also been important determinants in the Swedish context. The Social Democrats, and other parties on the left in Sweden, seemed especially affected by the conservative and neo-liberal winds that were blowing through the political arena after the breakdown in the East. The collapse of the Communist states in the East was interpreted in practice as a victory for market forces over centralised planning and steering. Today, the use of market forces in order to control the production and consumption of goods and services can be seenin a whole array of countries, even those that tolerate little democracy.

A number of social and civil factors can also be said to have influenced the changes in Sweden. Englund (1993) sees the changes in the Swedish education system as a shift from seeing education as a "public good" to a "private good". Citizens' rights are being strengthened and the role of the education system for the state is changing. Proponents for the reform claimed that parents and the general public were discontent with schools because they were ineffective, impossible to influence and too uniform and regulated. However, national surveys measuring the general public's confidence and trust in social institutions do not necessarily support these claims. The findings from a number of opinion surveys are summarised later in this article, in the section entitled "Attitudes to Choice and Independent Schools". Before the reform, there were no visible parent or student protests demanding increased school choice or more favourable conditions for independent schools. In fact, the rather weak response to new opportunities for choice, promoted by the use of school vouchers, supports the claim that the reform was ideologically motivated and not necessarily based upon the demands frior the grassroots.

Current Status of Independent Schools

In earlier reports (Miron, 1993, 1994), I have traced the changes in the independent schools during the period encompassing the two years prior to and following the introduction of the reform. While many of the trends were not clearly distinguishable then, we can now – after four years – see a number of trends emerging.

Given the favourable conditions for independent schools, one would have expected a large shift in enrolments from municipal to independent schools. During the 1991/92 school year – prior to the introduction of school vouchers – there were 89 independent schools operating in the country with more than 8,337 enrolled students. Many of these schools were, actually, already subsidised by the government. During the 1995/96 school year, the number of independent schools at the compulsory level had increased to 238 and the number of students enrolled in these schools had increased to 20,247.

While these figures underscore the fact that the independent schools have more than doubled during a period of four years, the growth in relation to total national enrolments was very small. Enrolments in independent schools increased from 0.94 per cent to 2.1 per cent of the national enrolments during this period, while the number of independent schools at the compulsory level increased from 1.9 per cent of all the compulsory level schools in 1991/92 to 4.8 per cent during the 1995/96 school year.

Figure 1 illustrates the growth of independent schools, in terms of the number of schools and enrolled students, over the past five years. While the number of enrolled students has grown rather steadily, one can see that the growth of approved independent schools has been more affected by political changes. After the Social Democrats regained power at the end of 1994, the rate of increase of newly approved independent schools declined noticeably. This is likely to be due to the uncertainty regarding the future conditions for independent schools.

In 1993, a similar school voucher scheme was implemented for upper secondary schools (*gymnasium*). Independent schools with equivalent study programs to the upper secondary schools already existing in the municipality would receive funding, from the given municipality, based upon the number of students enrolled. Independent schools which complement the existing schools (i.e. with unique study programs not already available) could qualify for funding directly from the state. During the 1991/92 school year, there were 58 independent upper secondary schools with 4,590 students enrolled in them. This represented 9.7 per cent of all upper secondary schools in the country and 1.5 per cent of all students enrolled in upper secondary schools. During the 1995/96 school year, these figures increased to 70 independent upper secondary schools (10.9 per cent of country totals) with 7,200 students (2.3 per cent of country totals).

Compulsory Schools in Sweden

	SCHOOLS			STUDENTS		
	Independent	Country Total		Independent	Country Total	
Year	Number of Schools	Country Total	Percentage of All Schools	Number of Students	Country Total	Percentage of All Students
1990/91	63	4649	1.36	7884	881523	0.89
1991/92	89	4697	1.89	8337	884449	0.94
1992/93	106	4745	2.23	9946	887375	1.12
1993/94	164	4824	3.40	13556	893799	1.52
1994/95	217	4900	4.43	17273	916661	1.88
1995/96	238	4934	4.82	20247	938869	2.16

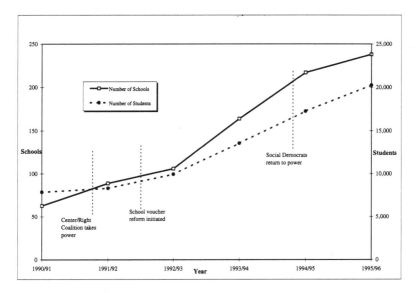

Figure 1. The growth of independent compulsory level schools in Sweden (1990-1996).

The main changes in enrolments have occurred in the larger cities where most of the independent schools are found. More than 100 of the 288 municipalities in the country have no independent schools at all. Disparities in choice are increasing in Sweden, since very few independent schools are being established in rural or remote areas of the country, and the "free choice revolution" remains largely an urban phenomenon.

It should be pointed out, however, that a handful of independent schools have been established in rural areas. Owing to economic pressure, a number of municipalities have been forced to close small village schools that lack a sufficient number of students to make them efficient. The parents have resisted this, since they do not want their children bussed to a larger community. In a few cases, parents have reopened the local school as an independent school, thus forcing the municipality to reallocate resources for small and supposedly costly village schools.

Enrolments by School Type

The most common type of compulsory-level independent school has a special pedagogical approach (e.g. Montessori or Waldorf schools). During the 1995/96 school year, they contain 33 per cent of all students in compulsory-level independent schools. Montessori schools, alone, are the fastest growing category of independent schools. Independent schools with a general profile, that is equivalent to the municipal schools, form the next largest category with 25.5 per cent of all independent students. Schools with religious profiles increased very rapidly just after the reform was initiated, but are now expanding more slowly than other school types. Currently, they contain 16.9 per cent of all students in independent schools. During the last few years, a number of Islamic schools have also joined the religious school category which is otherwise largely dominated by Christian schools. Schools with a language or ethnic profile comprise 8.5 per cent of enrolments, and international schools have 7 per cent of the enrolments in independent schools. Schools with a special subject profile contain 7.5 per cent, residential schools have 0.9 per cent of all students and a category of schools referred to as "other" contains 0.5 per cent of all the students in compulsory level independent schools.

School Fees

Many independent schools still require school fees. Although these fees are usually not large, they can restrict some families from choosing them, especially when they have more than one child. While there were apparent decreases in student fees after the introduction of school vouchers for independent schools, one would expect that there would be substantially greater decreases. Some of the independent schools actually increased their fees at the same time they began receiving school vouchers. Of the 86 schools which reported information on student fees in September 1992 (just after the introduction of school vouchers), nearly half of them still had school fees, 38 per cent had no fees, and 16 per cent had voluntary fees (Miron, 1993). Since then, school fees have decreased further or disappeared in most of the independent schools, particularly in those that are newly established. The National Agency for Education has found that school fees were unreasonably high in more than a dozen cases, and the schools have been requested to reduce them. The average annual school fee for independent schools receiving public financing was 1,300 Swedish crowns (equivalent to around $US 200) during the 1994/95 school year. This comprises about 3 per cent of the total resources of the independent schools. Estimates from the 1994/95 school year (National Agency for Education, 1995) noted that municipal and independent schools had about the same annual per-student costs, just over 47,000 Swedish crowns (approximately $US 7,100).

Attitudes to Choice and Independent Schools

Opinion surveys conducted in the 1980s and 1990s indicate that the Swedish public was rather confident in the education system (see Petersson et al, 1989; Holmberg & Weibull, 1992; and SIFO surveys from 19841991 summarised in a report by the National Agency for Education, 1993). The results from these studies indicate that the general public is pleased with the education system and has a high degree of confidence in schools, even though they do not believe they have a reasonable possibility to influence the activities in the school. In fact, these studies indicated that the level of public confidence in schools has been stable over a number of years, even while public confidence in many other social institutions declined. The research findings cannot be said to be conclusive, however. A survey of 12 OECD countries (OECD, 1995) found that the Swedish public had the lowest level of confidence in the teaching of subjects and the development of qualities in their schools.

In the late 1980s and early 1990s, the general public was increasingly positive towards privatisation and the existence of private alternatives, including in the school sector. In 1990, a balance point was reached when about 36 per cent of the persons questioned were positive towards more private schools and 35 per cent were negative. Interestingly, just when the Conservative government was preparing to improve the conditions for private alternatives, the general public's belief in private alternatives declined (Holmberg & Weibull, 1992).

An opinion survey conducted at the end of 1992 and the beginning of 1993 indicated that parents, as a whole, were positive towards school choice and the existence of independent schools. (TEMO, 1993). The survey results are based upon interviews with approximately 1,000 parents. The findings presented in the following three paragraphs are based upon the TEMO survey.

Sixty per cent of the parents felt that school choice was important. Around 50 per cent felt that choice of teacher was also important. Likewise, 60 per cent of the parents felt that competition between schools was good, and around 50 per cent felt that the presence of more independent schools was good. These results do not differ much from other countries. Parents believe they should have the right to choose. Nevertheless, even when given the right to choose a school, few parents exercise this right. Only 7 per cent of the parents questioned in the survey had actually applied to another municipal or independent school.

The parents surveyed believed that school choice would lead to a number of improvements, such as: (i) make teachers work harder (60 per cent); (ii) improve the quality of instruction (50 per cent); and (iii) induce parents to be more engaged and increase their influence (60 per cent). Nonetheless, the parents were far from convinced that school choice could lead to greater student influence.

Many of the parents believed that negative consequences could result from school choice. Two thirds of the parents felt that "élite schools" would arise, and 60 per cent felt that some schools would have to be closed as a result of school choice. Finally, 44 per cent of the parents felt that school choice would increase the overall costs for schooling, while a slightly larger percentage did not believe that this would be the case.

Why Do They Choose?

The quality of instruction and the social climate in the school were deemed by parents to be among the most important factors when choosing a school (National Agency for Education, 1993). After these factors, the parents noted the following three factors, listed in order of importance: convenience and proximity of the school; presence of their children's friends; and specific profile of the school. Around one-third of the parents felt that a specific pedagogic orientation (i.e. Montessori, Waldorf, etc.) was important in choosing a school, while only around 5 per cent of the parents felt that a specific religious orientation was important.

Access to information is important in determining attitudes to choice and the degree to which parents actively made choices. Three-quarters of the parents surveyed in the study had heard about the possibility of school choice. The mass media were the most important source of information for parents in regard to this issue. Only 16 per cent of the parents reported that they had received information directly from the local municipality. About half of the parents said they had some knowledge about which alternatives were available to them. Around 40 per cent of the parents felt that there was an alternative school available within a reasonable distance and that they had a sufficient amount of information in order to make a choice.

Parents with university training and parents living in urban areas were better informed about school choice than other parents. Additionally, they were more positive towards competition between schools and the existence of independent schools. Likewise they were more likely to choose another school for their child than the one assigned.

Attitudes to school choice and the proportion of parents actively making choices vary greatly among municipalities. The results from a number of municipal case studies (National Agency for Education, 1993) attributed these differences to a number of conditions or factors, including differences in the amount and quality of information available to parents and the availability of a diversity of schools within reasonable distance. Differences could also be traced to ideological differences in the municipal governments as well as differences in the local traditions in the municipalities.

Negative Consequences of the Reforms

Increasing Segregation by Ethnic Group, Social Class and Ability Level

Concerns have arisen about segregation by ethnic grouping, by social class and by ability level. There is today some evidence to support this conjecture. Growing segregation and increasing disparities among schools are becoming increasingly apparent, particularly in and around the three larger urban areas of the country. The municipalities in these areas accommodate most of the independent schools, and they also have the most favourable conditions for choice between public schools.

In the urban areas with high concentrations of immigrants – and with choice also possible between municipal schools – ethnic sorting is being intensified by school choice. Children of Swedish origin are moving from schools which have a large number of immigrant students. Likewise, children of well-educated immigrants are starting to move from schools predominately containing immigrants. Nevertheless, extreme examples of ethic sorting are only found in a few schools, and in the country as a whole not much has actually changed.

Some opponents of the reform fear that independent schools can establish rules for entry that imply that they can get precisely the number and type of children they want. This is exemplified in a few schools with high fees, and in one particular school that wishes to use entrance tests (entrance tests are not allowed, although this is being appealed and tested). Such measures as these make it possible to maintain a rather homogeneous group in the school. The public schools cannot do this; on the contrary, they are obliged to accept all children, and they must provide schools or arrange access to schools in sparsely populated and remote areas. There are merits in choice for consumers. However, there is a danger when applying market mechanisms to schools that the producers of education begin to choose the consumers, instead of vice versa.

Owing to the higher costs and greater resource needs, schools may simply refuse to accept children with special learning needs or disabilities. Enrolments in segregated special schools has been increasing in recent years, perhaps because the public schools do not have the resources to provide the quality support services that have been available in the past. Some parents, whose children have learning disabilities, have even established their own independent school since they felt that the public schools could not provide the quality support services needed to guarantee their children's successful participation.

Similar reforms in other countries have awoken the old issue of selectivity versus a common comprehensive school; yet, in Sweden, it is difficult – or too early – to say whether this will become a disputed issue as a result of the reforms over the last several years.

Children with Special Learning Needs

Internationally, Sweden has been considered a leader for its progressive and quality education for children with disabilities and/or special learning needs. Yet, increasing competition and demands for efficiency are encroaching upon the position of these children in the schools. With the further decentralisation of financial matters, school leaders and municipal authorities are induced to make cuts in the services for children with special needs in light of the high costs involved. After all, the reforms deal not only with choice but also with efficiency, and children who require extra resources are liabilities.

While cuts are being made in all areas, support for children with difficulties and special learning needs seems to be the most affected. Teachers for children with special learning needs and home language teachers have been most affected by the cuts in teachers' ranks. A report from Stockholm School Administration (1992) noted that 80 special teacher positions (nearly a quarter of all special teachers in the municipality of Stockholm) had been eliminated, half-class sessions were cut back, and the number of hours devoted to speech therapy were cut in half. Reports such as this bring the issue of segregation by ability into the foreground, and mark the reversal of another long-standing Swedish education policy. Interestingly, the parents interviewed in the TEMO survey (1993) did not believe that children with difficulties would be negatively affected by the reforms. Forty-four per cent of the parents felt, for example, that school choice would lead to better conditions for children with difficulties or special needs, while only around 25 per cent of the parents felt that school choice would worsen conditions for them.

The government-appointed representative of children and youth in Sweden (*Barnombudsmannen*) has recently warned the government about the difficult situation of children (*Barnombudsmannen*, 1996). The stress and pressure from high unemployment, cuts in social benefits, etc., are most visible in the declining psycho-social well-being of children and youth. At the same time as the needs of children and youth are increasing, the support services for them are being reduced. This has occurred, not necessarily because of school choice, but because of budget cuts and frugal decisions made by school leaders.

Increased Efficiency or Just Plain Budget Cuts?

There has been extensive reductions of costs for compulsory-level schooling during the last four years. These reductions are mainly due to cuts from the state and the municipal governments and are not necessarily the result of increased efficiency. Between 1991 and 1994, there was a 17 per cent reduction in instruction costs alone (*Dagens Nyheter*, 1995) Concretely, the effects of these cuts can be seen in the decreasing number of teachers in the schools over the past five years, even while national enrolments are increasing, owing to the entrance of large age cohorts into the school system.

Besides the cuts in state and municipal funds for education, the budgets for the municipal schools are also being constrained because of the reallocation of resources to independent schools. In Stockholm, for example, the additional annual costs based on the number of independent schools in 1991 was estimated to be 31 million Swedish crowns (SOU, 1992:38). One study found that the additional costs for the municipalities during the 1993/94 school year was estimated to be 200 million Swedish crowns (Social Democratic Parliamentary Group, 1993).

The economic pressure on the schools is great, and many of the difficult decisions on how and where to make the cuts have been delegated to school principals. This has resulted in some drastic and unusual measures in order to deal with reduced budgets. A number of schools, for example, have had their textbooks paid for by sponsors who are allowed to advertise in the books. The advertisements are collected at the end of the book and, in a few instances, more pages are devoted to advertisements than to instructional text. Some schools have cut back on health services. Recently, it was discovered that a number of schools did not have the resources to pay for the vaccinations that are usually administered by school health services. Aside from the above-mentioned examples of drastic reactions, hardly a day passes without the media reporting on some improvement or adaptation in the schools. These innovations and changes have been the focus of a number of recent Master's theses at the Institute of International Education in Stockholm. The most noteworthy is Enquist (1995). The kindling of dynamic and innovative change – particularly in the municipal schools – is perhaps the greatest impact of the reforms. After all, parents are choosing public schools considerably more often than independent schools.

Conclusion

Since the end of the 1970s and early 1980s, there are growing demands on national education systems for more efficiency and improved quality. Because of the adverse economic setting, the resources available for education are diminishing. Simultaneously, there is increasing interdependency and competition among countries, which have made political leaders aware of the need to increase the human capital of their workforces in order to make their existing industries more competitive and to make them more capable of developing and manufacturing new technologies. In Sweden, both the Social Democrats and the Conservative opposition agree upon the need for increased efficiency and quality. The difference between them is the nature and manner in which they wish to reform the education system.

On the one hand, the Conservatives have a tendency to consider the national education system as being too lethargic, difficult and complex to change. Thus, they prefer to circumvent the public system and invest in alternative forms of schools outside of the control of existing bureaucracies (both at the central level and the municipal level). The school voucher reform of 1992 was typical, since its focus was to improve the working conditions and financial resources for independent schools. After four years, however, the independent schools have only increased from one per cent to just over two per cent of the national enrolments. Their presence cannot be seen as directly affecting the overall efficiency and quality of the education system. Nonetheless, their presence constitutes a threat for the municipal schools and induces them to be more accountable.

Although there are sharp differences within the Social Democratic Party, as a whole they have tended to focus on decentralisation to municipalities and schools. Critical changes require professional involvement and the greatest source of experienced, professional and "organised" educators in the existing public school system. Therefore, the emphasis is to devolve authority, to free the structures and the steering of the schools and to encourage the professionals to innovate and to cope with declining budgets.

Nonetheless, additional time will be needed to see if the negative affects of the reforms, such as increasing segregation and disparities between and within schools, will outweigh the increased efficiency. Likewise, more time will be needed to see if quality improvements have been made or if the schools have simply scaled down their activities in relation to the decreasing resources available. In other words, it is as yet too soon to see what the long-term results of the short-sighted market-oriented reforms will have in Sweden.

References

Barnombudsmannen (1996) Tänk om ... Rapport från barnens myndighet. Stockholm: Barnombudsmannen.

Dagens Nyheter (1995) Kommuner spara på undervisning, September 9, 1995. Stockholm: Dagens Nyheter.

Daun, H. & Miron, G. (1994) Restructuring Education in Europe: a comparative study of changes in response to European integration and pressure from economic, political and social-cultural factors. Research Proposal. Stockholm: Institute of International Education.

Englund, T. (1993) Education for Public or Private Good, in G. Miron (Ed.) *Towards Free Choice and Market-Oriented Schools: problems and promises.* Stockholm: National Agency for Education.

Enquist, S. (1995) Accountable School Development in Sweden: the Matteus school experience. Unpublished MA thesis. Stockholm: Institute of International Education.

Government Bill 1990/91:115. "Vissa skollagsfrågor m.m." Regeringens proposition 1990/91:115.

Government Bill 1991/92:95. "Valfrihet och fristående skolor." Regeringens proposition 1991/92:95.

Holmberg, S. & Weibull, L. (1992) Trendbrott? in S. Holmberg & L. Weibull (Eds.) *Trendbrott? SOM-undersökningen 1991.* SOM rapport 8, Göteborg: Political Science Institute and the Institute for Journalism, Media and Communication, Göteborg University.

Marklund, S. 1986. Fristående skolor och alternative pedagogik, *Skolöverstyrelsen Rapport,* 86:23. Stockholm: The National Board of Education.

Miron, G. (1993) *Choice and the Use of Market Forces: Swedish Education Reforms for the 1990s.* Studies in Comparative and International Education No. 25. Stockholm: Institute of International Education.

Miron, G. (1994) Valfrihet och marknadskrafter i det svenska utbildningsstystemet, *Didactica Minima,* 28, pp. 226.

National Agency for Education (1993) *Val av skola: rapport om valfrihet inom skolpliktens ram läsåret 1992/93.* Stockholm: Skolverket.

National Agency for Education (1995) *Jämförelsetal för skolhuvudmän: organisation, resurser och resultat.* Stockholm: Skolverket.

OECD (1995) *Education at a Glance: OECD indicators.* Paris: Centre for Educational Research and Innovation, OECD.

Petersson, O., Westholm, A. & Blomberg, G. (1989) *Medborgarnas Makt.* Stockholm: Carlsson's Publishing.

Social Democratic Parliamentary Group (1993) Spara och slösa – kommmunal och privat skola idag. Stockholm: Socialdemokratiska riksdagsgruppen.

SOU. 1992:38. Fristående skolor. Bidrag och elevavgifter. Statens offentliga utredningar (SOU) 1992:38. Stockholm: Allmänna Förlaget.

Stockholm School Administration (1992) De Stora små förlorarna. Situationen för elever med svarigheter och särskilda behov. Stockholm: Stockholms Skolor.

TEMO. 1993. Det fria skolvalen – en attitydundersökning bland föräldrar till barn i grundskolan för Skolverket. Solna: Testhuset marknad opinion (TEMO).

Oxford Studies in Comparative Education, Vol. 6(1), 1996

School Choice and the Quasi-market in England and Wales

GEOFFREY WALFORD

Introduction

Over the last two decades the state-maintained educational system of England and Wales has been subjected to a plethora of changes that have been justified in terms of introducing 'market discipline' into education by giving parents a greater choice of school. These changes include the introduction of the Assisted Places Scheme in 1980; the granting of greater opportunity for parents to 'express a preference' for particular state maintained schools following the Education Act of 1980; the development of City Technology Colleges from 1986; the 1988 restructuring of the education system through grant maintained schools, local management of schools and open enrolment; the 1993 Act's even greater emphasis on choice and diversity; and the development of 'specialisms' within comprehensive schools. All of these policies have important implications for educational equity.

Early Concepts of Choice

Historically, choice of school in England and Wales has been mainly available only to those families able and willing to pay high fees for private schools. The private sector is smaller than in most industrial countries, as most of the Church of England and Roman Catholic schools were incorporated into the state-maintained sector following the 1944 Education Act. In consequence, although there is considerable diversity within the sector, private schools are generally more academically and socially selective than in other countries, and now serve just 7.5 per cent of the school age population (Whitty et al,

1989; Walford, 1991). Prior to 1975 some highly able children were selected to enter specific private grammar schools on scholarships. These 'Direct Grant' schools were officially part of the private sector and charged fees, but they entered into agreements with central and local governments to provide a certain number of free or subsidised places to children passing academic entrance examinations. For those who passed the examinations, there was thus the choice of whether or not to accept the place offered, but the majority of families were unable to contemplate using the private sector. Within the state-maintained sector there was very little choice of school.

The 1944 Education Act for England and Wales included clauses relating to parental preferences, but they were designed to ensure that parents could indicate their wishes with regard to the religious denomination of schools that had just been brought into the state system, and were not intended to give choice between individual schools (see Walford, 1994a). The allocation of children to schools of the same type was under the control of the Local Education Authorities (LEAs) and was usually done by means of residential catchment areas for each school. While some parents gradually began to question and appeal against the allocation of their child to a particular school, most were prepared to accept their catchment area school when there was an obvious shortage of accommodation. However, in England and Wales the number of 10 year-olds reached its peak in 1975, and there was a decline of some 30 per cent in the years until 1987. It is this dramatic demographic change that does most to explain the increased interest in parental choice of school in Britain in the late 1970s and into the 1980s. When this demographic feature was combined with the Conservative government's growing belief in 'the market' as having greater efficiency and effectiveness than central or local democratic planning, a lethal cocktail was mixed.

From the mid 1970s, it became obvious that many schools had spare capacity, and the then Labour government was faced with a growing demand from parents to have the right to choose a particular school for their children. An Education Bill was produced in 1978 which was intended to allow greater choice in a context where ultimate control was still retained by the LEAs. It recognised the need for some school closures and for LEAs to be able to plan local provision to ensure high educational standards for all children.

Choice after 1979

A General Election was called in 1979 before the Labour Education Bill became law, but Mrs Thatcher's newly elected Conservative government rapidly moved to implement its own version of parental choice through the 1980 Education Act. Much of the Act was similar to the 1978 Bill proposed by Labour, simply because it aimed to solve the same problems, but the ideological emphasis was shifted towards moving schools into the market place and generating more competition between schools. From 1982 parents were given the right to 'express a preference' for a school of their choice, and the LEA was obliged to take this preference into account. However, the Act still gave LEAs considerable powers so that they could manage falling school rolls and plan the overall provision of school places in their areas. It allowed the benefits of the community as a whole to override the benefits to individual parents by giving LEAs the right to refuse parents' preferences if this would lead to some less-popular schools having unviable numbers.

Stillman & Maychell (1986; Stillman, 1986) have shown that the effect of this legislation throughout England and Wales was extremely variable. Some LEAs tried to encourage parental choice, while others endeavoured to restrict it. Those offering minimal choice justified their behaviour in terms of catchment area schools fostering better links with the local community. They also argued that catchment areas ensured that the LEA could engage in long-term planning and hence benefit from the most efficient and effective use of resources. There were many examples of both Conservative and Labour LEAs offering only very restricted choice.

More Choice in the Private Sector

The perceived academic success of private schools, which were seen as thriving in a competitive market, was one of the factors that encouraged successive Conservative governments to introduce a quasi-market into the state-maintained sector. But the first stage was to introduce a scheme designed to replace the former Direct Grant arrangements that had been phased out by the Labour government from 1975. The Assisted Places Scheme, introduced in the 1980 Education Act for England and Wales, was officially designed to "give able children a wider range of educational opportunities' by giving 'help with tuition fees at independent schools to parents who could not otherwise afford them" (DES, 1985). In practice, it not only helps individual parents and children, but gives substantial financial and ideological support to the private schools themselves. About twelve per cent of secondary pupils in the private sector are now supported through the Assisted Places Scheme, and the scale of the scheme has been recently increased. Individual schools are allocated a set number of places each year and are able to fill these places using their own selection methods.

The major study of the Assisted Places Scheme conducted by Edwards, Fitz & Whitty (1989) drew on national statistical data on the allocation and take-up of places from 1981 to 1987, and extensive case study data drawn from interviews with pupils, parents and headteachers from the private schools involved and from state maintained schools. Not unexpectedly with a scheme where parents initially have to be aware of the possibility of financial help and then determined enough to apply and be interviewed by the schools, there was a severe social class bias in the children selected. The authors show that, while about a third of the pupils were from single parent families, many of them had existing links with the private sector. There was a low participation rate from manual working-class families, and from families of some ethnic minorities, particularly those of Afro-Caribbean origin. Although the scheme is means-tested, about one-third of children on Assisted Places had parents with above average incomes. They suggest that a considerable proportion of Assisted Place holders came from submerged middle-class backgrounds already well endowed with cultural capital. It was also very noticeable that there were considerably more boys benefiting from the scheme than girls.

It is also notable that when the scheme was introduced there was no ideological linkage between the desire to increase choice and that of raising overall educational standards. Indeed, the APS was predicated on the belief that some state schools were so bad that the only hope for academically able children was to remove them from these schools and place them in private schools. At this stage here was no suggestion that the introduction of this new 'quasi-market' mechanism might lead to any improvement in state schools.

Choice in the Mid 1980s

As the 1980s progressed two successive Conservative Governments pushed through a series of privatizations of state owned enterprises and services (Walford, 1990). These moves were seen as part of a general policy of 'rolling back the frontiers of the state' and encouraging market competition wherever possible. The rigours of the market were seen as the way by which higher quality and greater efficiency were to be achieved. Inevitably, education services were also the subject of similar measures, and it is at this point that strong links began to be made between choice, the market and raising educational standards.

At the 1986 Conservative Party Annual Conference that preceded the 1987 General Election, a particularly dramatic policy was announced under the guise of giving greater parental choice. The Secretary of State for Education and Science announced the creation of a pilot network of 20 City Technology Colleges to cater for 11 to 18 year olds in selected inner-city areas. These were to be private schools, run by educational trusts with close links with industry and commerce. The Governing Bodies of these schools were to include many representatives from industry and commerce but to exclude both parent and teacher governors. The CTCs would charge no fees, but sponsors would be expected to cover the extra costs involved in providing a highly technological curriculum and would make substantial contributions to both capital and current expenditure. They were to select children with a broad range of academic abilities from a defined catchment area. Significantly, these new schools were also supposed to act as 'beacons of excellence' for nearby LEA schools and thus raise educational standards overall.

The desire to increase technological education was a major feature of the plan, but many public political speeches at the time showed that CTCs were also designed to encourage inequality of educational provision, increase competition, reintroduce selection, weaken the comprehensive system and reduce the powers of the LEAs. As the title of the promotional booklet, *City Technology Colleges: a new choice of school* (DES, 1986), makes clear, this was all to be justified and legitimized through the ideology of increased parental choice, and the idea that greater choice within an educational quasi-market would improve educational standards for all.

The results of the CTC initiative have not been as planned. There was fierce opposition to the scheme from LEAs, teachers' unions and some local action groups. More unexpectedly, many involved in industry and commerce were also against the idea and expressed the belief that technological education was better served through their involvement in many schools rather than through concentration of their efforts and resources on a small number of CTCs. The CTCs have proved much more expensive to establish than was first thought, and sponsors have provided only about 20 per cent of the capital expenditure and little of the current expenditure. At the first CTC at Kingshurst, Solihull, for example, sponsors provided £2.1 million towards the capital costs of establishing this new private educational trust school, but the state has given more than £8 million towards capital costs and will provide the vast majority of the ongoing current expenditure.

All of the CTCs are required to provide education for children of different abilities who are wholly or mainly drawn from the area in which the school is situated. The CTC at Kingshurst selects children from a tightly defined catchment area which includes eight LEA secondary schools, and is thus in direct competition with these other schools for pupils. Parents are required to apply for admission to the CTC on behalf of their child. The child takes a simple non-verbal reasoning test which is used to ensure that children are selected with a range of abilities broadly representative of those who apply. They are also interviewed with a parent. Parents and the child also have to state that they intend the child to continue in full-time education until age 18. The study by Walford & Miller (1991) showed that the college took great care to ensure that it was taking children with a wide ability range, but the whole entry procedure means that selection is based on the degree of motivation of parents and children instead. Children and families where there is a low level of interest in education simply do not apply.

In interviews, heads and teachers in the nearby LEA schools claimed that the CTC was selecting those very parents who have the most interest in their children's education, and those children who are most keen and enthusiastic. They argued that the CTC was selecting children who, while they might not be particularly academically able, had special skills and interests in sport, art, drama or other activities. These children were seen as invigorating the atmosphere of any school, providing models for other children, and being rewarding for teachers to teach. Heads and teachers in nearby schools thus saw their schools as having been impoverished by the

CTC's selection of these well-motivated pupils. They saw the CTC as having only a negative effect on their schools.

The present reality is thus far from the optimistic future presented in 1986 and, in spite of substantial government support, there are still only 15 Colleges. But the symbolic significance of the CTCs is disproportionate to the number of pupils involved. Fundamentally, the CTC idea made it clear that the Government wished to develop a more market-based educational system based on inequality of provision and the selection of children for those schools with the best facilities, funding and support. The CTCs may have been a faltering start to this change, but the idea rapidly led to more radical changes.

Choice and the 1988 Education Reform Act

The 1988 Education Reform Act for England and Wales introduced a wide range of ideas designed to hasten market processes within education (Walford, 1994a). Through the introduction of grant maintained schools and in the interlinked ideas of local management of schools and open enrolment, the major thrust of the Act was designed to increase competition between schools and to encourage parents to make choices between schools. Funding to individual schools is now largely related directly to pupil numbers, and schools have their own delegated budgets. Popular schools gain extra funding as they attract more pupils, while less popular schools lose funding as their numbers decline. LEAs have lost much of their power to give extra support in areas of special need or to temporarily adjust funding to particular schools to ensure that future needs are met. At a time of falling school rolls, this means that the choice of which schools will close is left largely to the summation of the decisions of existing parents. The needs of future parents, or the society as a whole, are forgotten.

Encouraged by large grants from central government, the number of schools seeking grant maintained status is now increasing rapidly. Fitz et al (1993) have shown that many of the schools involved in the early stages had been part of local authority schemes designed to close or reorganize schools to deal with falling school rolls. They show that many of the schools that have achieved grant maintained status were identified by their former LEAs for closure or reorganization. In several cases this has led to whole LEA reorganization schemes having to be reworked and considerable waste of public funding as schools still continue to operate with very low pupil numbers. Almost two-thirds of their local authority correspondents reported that their local authority's reorganisation plans had been either abandoned or temporarily shelved after schools had decided to opt out. They argue that the individualistic decisions of single schools to opt out were inhibiting the viability of whole local schemes of provision, and resulting in negative financial and educational consequences for the other schools in the area.

Both grant maintained schools and open enrolment were designed to increase competition between schools and to encourage parents to make choices between schools. However, once schools become oversubscribed, it is the schools that are able to select children and families rather than families being able to choose a school. Early research evidence on grant maintained schools is mixed. One study (Fitz et al, 1993), whilst agreeing that grant maintained schools were increasingly popular and that a large proportion of grant maintained schools were selective, argued that (at the time of the research) there was little evidence for a widespread return of a selective system. In contrast, a second study (Bush et al, 1993) showed that 30 per cent of the supposedly comprehensive schools in their grant maintained sample were using covert selection and one had introduced a selection examination. The authors argued that the grant maintained policy was leading to the development of a two-tier system. What is interesting is that, in spite of heavy capital investment and continued additional current expenditure, there is little evidence that grant maintained schools offer much that is distinctively different from that provided in local authority schools. Often parents and pupils see no difference between grant maintained schools and the local authority schools apart from better facilities and greater attention to the symbols of academic elitism such as logos and school uniforms. Where they are perceived as different, it is that they offer a 'better' quality education of the same sort as before (Fitz et al, 1993; Bush et al, 1993). However, since both research studies were conducted, two comprehensive grant maintained schools have successfully applied for a 'change in character' to become fully academically selective grammar schools. One has become selective by aptitude for technology, and nine others have been granted permission to select up to 50 per cent of their intake.

Changes in the admissions criteria which involve this degree of selection require Department for Education authorization following a full consultation process, but in mid-1993 new DFE guidelines on admissions announced that all schools were to be allowed to specialise and to select up to 10 per cent of their intake on the basis of abilities in such areas as music, art, sport and technology without any need for official approval. The Government argued that specialisation need not lead to selection, but once there are more applications than places, selection must inevitably increase. Equally worrying is the growth of 'adverse selection' where 'mistakes' in initial selection procedures are increasingly rectified through temporary or permanent exclusions.

Further quasi-market mechanisms were introduced through the 1993 Education Act. First, grant maintained schools and voluntary aided schools were encouraged to appoint sponsor governors from business and become Technology Colleges specialising in science, technology and mathematics. So far, 150 schools have been able to find at least £100,000 from sponsors, and in return the schools have received more than matching extra resources from the DFE. Such extra resources to a limited number of schools can lead to substantial differences between the learning environments of neighbouring schools. While overt selection is not necessarily introduced, self-selection will operate in a similar way to the original City Technology Colleges. More recently, the Secretary of State for Education, Gillian Shephard, extended the scheme to include specialist language schools and opened the scheme to a broader range of secondary schools.

Second, the 1993 Education Act began to encourage the supply side of the quasi-market. While the 1988 Act introduced grant maintained schools, it did nothing to encourage the development of entirely new schools. In contrast, the 1993 Education Act made it possible for the governors of existing private schools or groups of independent sponsors to apply to the Secretary of State to establish sponsored grant maintained schools. These schools may be based on particular religious or philosophical beliefs such as Islam, Hinduism or evangelical Christianity, or may be designed to follow particular teaching methods or subject specialisms. However, to have a chance of acceptance sponsors have to be able to find at least 15 per cent of the funding for buildings and land, and be prepared to accept the regulations and constraints applicable to all other grant maintained schools including following the National Curriculum.

The reluctance of the government to deal with the supply-side is an indication of the ambiguity of its policy on choice and the market. I have shown elsewhere (Walford, 1995a, b & c) that small groups representing existing private evangelical Christian schools and Muslim schools campaigned over the late 1980s and early 1990s for the right to become faith-based grant maintained schools. The development of the supply side is thus the result of a genuine demand for diversity within the state sector. However, government has shown itself slow to support such real diversity (Walford, 1996, 1997). It has made the process of gaining support very difficult and costly so that, so far, only two existing private schools have become grant maintained and no entirely new schools have been started. None of the schools involved in the Campaign has managed to make the transition to grant maintained status.

Reasons for Choice and Who Makes the Choice

Prior to the 1980 Education Act, most research on choice in England and Wales had concentrated on the private sector (see Johnson, 1990; Walford, 1990). One of the most important findings of these studies of choice is the wide range of different factors seen as important. However, in her study of parents of boys in Headmasters' Conference schools, Fox (1985) found that the most frequently voiced criteria for choice were related to the perception that these schools could produce better academic results and develop character through discipline. However, the distance of the school from the parental home was still an important factor, even where the child boarded.

Following the 1980 Education Act and, in particular, the 1988 Education Reform Act, there has been a growing number of research projects into choice of school in the state-maintained sector. The focus has often been on the reasons for choosing a particular school, and it has been shown that parents often give greater value to 'process' rather than 'product' criteria (Elliott, 1982). 'Process' criteria involve factors indicative of the capacity for human relationships such as the happiness of the child, whilst 'product' criteria refer to outcome such as examination results. Studies carried out by Alston (1985), Boulton & Coldron (1989), Woods (1992), and Webster et al (1993) have all shown that 'parents are just as, if not more concerned with 'process' issues than measured outcomes when choosing schools' (Webster et al, 1993: 18). Other studies reporting similar findings include those by Hunter (1991), West (1992a, 1992b) and David et al (1994).

A typical example of this type of research is a small-scale study of parents of children in Sheffield primary schools about to move to secondary conducted by Boulton & Coldron (1989; Coldron & Boulton, 1991). Using a questionnaire returned by over 200 parents and interviews with 16 families, they found the most important factors influencing choice were the nearness of the school and the future attendance at the school of the child's siblings and friends. They found that parents ranked very highly the child's feelings of security and happiness in a new school environment in their choice of school. As a result, there was a very strong relationship between many parents' wishes for their child to be happy and the prioritizing of the preferences expressed by the child.

It would appear that the recent introduction of published 'league tables' of examination results has done little to reduce the influence of children's views on parents. In a small-scale interview study conducted in early 1993. Webster et al (1993) found that 69 per cent of their sample of parents rated the views of their children as 'very important' to them in their choice of school. A further 13 per cent rated their children's views as 'important'. Interestingly, three-quarters of their respondents stated that the published examination figures for the schools were unimportant in their decision-making. Only 18 per cent stated that they had been an important part of the process, while 22 per cent registered very strong negative reactions to the official figures.

More recent work by David et al (1994) and Carroll & Walford (1996a) has suggested an increase in the emphasis given to examination results by parents, but what is fascinating about the results of so many of these studies where the parents are questioned before the child enters secondary school, is that parents appear to give a high priority to the wishes of their children. At the time the choice is actually made, parents appear to give high status to the wishes of their ten-year- old sons and daughters. After the event, parents may rationalize their decision in terms of the criteria they believe the researcher might want to hear, but before the event, they are prepared to admit that their child's happiness in attending a particular school is an extremely important factor. Moreover, there are indications that there are systematic variations in the degree of legitimacy that parents accord to their children's views. Edwards et al (1989), for example, found the most striking difference between parents of able children at LEA comprehensive schools and those of Assisted Places Scheme children in private schools, was the extent to which they considered their child's desire to keep with friends. Those who chose the private sector for their children were more likely to ignore their children's wishes. Some delegation of responsibility has also been found in a small-scale study of children in two urban junior schools in Northern England conducted by Thomas & Dennison (1991). In that study of 72 children, 60 per cent claimed that they made their own choice of secondary school. Interviews with a sample of parents confirmed that most gave their children the 'biggest say' in the choice, and that their main concern was with their children's happiness. Carroll & Walford (1996b) also found that, while there was no simple relationship, the child's voice was more likely to be heard in working-class rather than middle-class families.

Other research studies have focused more on the workings of the micro-market of schools. The studies by Ball and his colleagues have been particularly influential (Ball, 1993; Ball et al, 1995; Gewirtz et al, 1995). They interviewed a broad spectrum of parents who had recently decided which secondary school to send their child to, and examined in detail the ways in which various families responded to the market situation in which they found themselves. Ball argues that families are privileged or disadvantaged by the values that inform their conceptions of choice-making. Indeed, 'choice' is a socially and culturally constricted concept which has different meanings to different families. Government policy, he claims, is predicated on a consumerist vision that is most likely to be embraced by the middle class. Ball (1993: 4) argues that

> *the implementation of market reforms in education is essentially a class*
> *strategy which has as one of its major effects the reproduction of relative social*
> *class (and ethnic) advantages and disadvantages.*

Gewirtz et al's (1995) study of the workings of choice and the market since 1988 has examined in detail the way in which various families respond to the market situation they find themselves in. They identify three broad groups of parents, defined in terms of their position in relation to the market: the privileged/skilled choosers, the semi-skilled choosers and the disconnected; and they show the ways in which working-class or newly immigrant families may be disadvantaged in the market. They present a picture of a complex situation where patterns of choice are generated both by choice preferences and opportunities, and where reputation and desirability are played off against other factors. But they also show that the way in which parents play the market is strongly related to social class, and that working-class parents are much more likely than middle-class parents to see the child's views as decisive.

Gewirtz et al (1995) also indicate that, where curriculum specialisms are being introduced by schools, they are sometimes acting as selection mechanisms for high academic ability and middle-class children. In particular, the development of specialisms such as dance or music indirectly discriminates against working class children, and allows schools a greater chance to select what they deem to be 'appropriate' children. They show that, in practice, rather than schools becoming more diverse, the pressures of competition between schools leads to schools becoming more similar in what they offer, but within a hierarchy of perceived ability to offer advantage. They conclude that local hierarchies of schools are developing where resources flow from those children with greatest need to those with the least need.

Conclusion

One of the main justifications that has been used for introducing a market and giving greater choice of school is that it is anticipated that popular schools will thrive while unpopular ones close. However, obviously this can only occur at a time of falling school rolls. Once less popular schools have closed in line with the falling pupil population, those remaining will be full. Without over-capacity in schools, parents will quickly find that their choices are severely curtailed, and that it is the schools that choose which children to accept rather than the parents and children choosing a school.

The idea that a quasi-market leads to higher overall standards is based on the assumption that choice of school will be made by parents, and that these parents will be well informed. It is supposedly the 'bad' schools that close and the 'good' ones that expand. However, it has been shown that parents make choices on a broad range of criteria and that academic issues appear to feature quite low on their list or priorities. Moreover, recent evidence has shown that the child's wishes are of great importance to many parents, and that many parents appear to delegate the decision of choice of school entirely to their child.

It highly unlikely that the sum of many such choices will automatically lead to higher educational standards for all. Some children and families will undoubtedly benefit, but they will do so at a cost to others. Indeed, these studies suggest that, rather than raising overall standards as predicted, greater inequalities and a hierarchy of schools are likely to develop. The children of well-motivated, educated or wealthy families are more likely to make applications to the popular schools. These oversubscribed schools will select children on a diverse and unclear range of criteria, but in a way likely to be heavily skewed towards children from families already highly valuing education. These popular schools will thus improve further through the financial and cultural support of the parents and children selected. In contrast, children from families which do not value education highly will probably find themselves in schools at the bottom of the hierarchy with low levels of financial and parental support.

Some parents and children will be more concerned and better informed about the effectiveness of various schools than others. Some parents are more able to pay for the transport of their children to school, and some parents are more likely to impose their decision about schooling on their children. In practice, the ideology of the market has little to do with any desire to increase educational standards, but conceals and mystifies the government's desire to construct a hierarchy of schools with unequal provision, into which children can be fitted to best equip them for their preordained roles in society. As choices are made and pupils selected, the schools will become more differentiated. Some will be able to draw on parental financial support for new buildings and equipment or to pay for additional teachers and helpers. Other schools will not be so lucky.

Eventually, this continuum of schools will offer different educational and social experiences to pupils, and various children will be fitted into these schools through a process of mutual selection. The evidence that we already have about choice suggests that this process of mutual selection will probably be closely linked to social class and ethnicity, and discriminate in particular against working-class children and children of Afro-Caribbean descent. There is also likely to be greater segregation between social and ethnic groups and less mutual understanding. The pre-existing social and economic order of wealth and privilege is likely to be confirmed. In summary, the main purpose of the recent moves towards greater choice is not to build a more democratic and fair educational system but to rebuild a more differentiated educational system which will more closely aid social reproduction. The ideology of the market and choice acts to partially mask this process and, while it may allow a few individuals to benefit, the majority have much to lose.

Note

This chapter draws upon some material previously published in G. Walford (1994b) Educational choice, control and inequity, in D. Scott (Ed.) *Accountability and Control in Educational Settings* (London, Cassell).

References

Alston, C. (1985) *Secondary Transfer Project. Bulletin 3: the views of parents before transfer*. London: ILEA.

Ball, S. (1993) Education markets, choice and social class: the market as a class strategy in the UK and the USA, *British Journal of Sociology of Education*, 14, pp. 3-19.

Ball, S., Bowe, R., & Gewirtz, S. (1995) Circuits of schooling: a sociological exploration of parental choice of school in social class contexts, *Sociological Review*, 43, pp. 52-78.

Boulton, P. & Coldron, J. (1989) *The Pattern and Process of Parental Choice Project Report*. Sheffield: Sheffield City Polytechnic.

Bush, T., Coleman, M. & Glover, D. (1993) *Managing Autonomous Schools: the grant maintained experience.* London: Paul Chapman.

Carroll, S. & Walford, G. (1996a) Parents' responses to the school quasi-market, *Research Papers in Education* (forthcoming).

Carroll, S. & Walford, G. (1996b) The child's voice in school choice, *Educational Management and Administration* (forthcoming).

Coldron, J. & Boulton, P. (1991) Happiness as a criterion of parents' choice of school, *Journal of Education Policy*, 6, pp.169-178.

David, M., West, A. & Ribbens, J. (1994) *Mother's Intuition? Choosing Secondary Schools.* London: Falmer.

Department of Education and Science (1985) *Assisted Places at Independent Schools.* London: DES.

Department of Education and Science (1986) *City Technology Colleges: a new choice of school.* London: DES.

Edwards, T., Fitz, J. & Whitty, G. (1989) *The State and Private Education: an evaluation of the Assisted Places Scheme.* London: Falmer.

Elliott, J. (1982) How do parents choose and judge secondary schools? in R. McCormick (Ed.) *Calling Education to Account.* Milton Keynes: Open University Press.

Fox, I. (1985) *Private Schools and Public Issues.* London: Macmillan.

Fitz, J., Halpin, D. & Power, S. (1993) *Grant Maintained Schools.* London: Kogan Page.

Gewirtz, S., Ball, S.J. & Bowe, R. (1995) *Markets, Choice and Equity in Education.* Buckingham: Open University Press.

Hunter, J.B. (1991) Which school? A study of parents' choice of secondary school, *Educational Research*, 33, pp. 31-41.

Johnson, D. (1990) *Parental Choice in Education.* London: Unwin Hyman.

Stillman, A. (1986) (Ed.) *The Balancing Act of 1980: parents, politics and education.* Windsor: NFER/Nelson.

Stillman, A. & Maychell, K. (1986) *Choosing Schools: parents, LEAs and the 1980 Education Act.* Windsor: NFERNelson.

Thomas, A. & Dennison, B. (1991) Parental or pupil choice: who really decides in urban schools? *Educational Management and Administration*, 19, pp. 243-249.

Walford, G. (1990) *Privatization and Privilege in Education.* London: Routledge.

Walford, G. (1991) (Ed.) *Private Schools: tradition, change and diversity.* London: Paul Chapman.

Walford, G. (1994a) *Choice and Equity in Education.* London: Cassell.

Walford, G. (1994b) Educational choice, control and inequity in D. Scott (Ed.) *Accountability and Control in Educational Settings.* London: Cassell.

Walford, G. (1995a) The Christian schools campaign: a successful educational pressure group? *British Educational Research Journal*, 21, pp. 451-464.

Walford, G. (1995b) The Northbourne amendments: is the House of Lords a garbage can? *Journal of Education Policy*, 10, pp. 413-425.

Walford, G. (1995c) *Educational Politics: pressure groups and faith-based schools.* Aldershot: Avebury.

Walford, G. (1996) Diversity and choice in school education: an alternative view, *Oxford Review of Education*, 22, pp. 143-154.

Walford, G. (1997) Sponsored grant maintained schools: extending the franchise? *Oxford Review of Education*, 23, 1.

Walford, G. & Miller, H. (1991) *City Technology College*. Buckingham: Open University Press.

Webster, A., Owen, G. & Crome, D. (1993) *School Marketing: Making it easy for parents to select your school.* Bristol: Avec Designs.

West, A. (1992a) Factors affecting choice of school for middle class parents: implications for marketing, *Educational Management and Administration*, 29, pp. 213-221.

West, A. (1992b) *Choosing Schools: why do parents opt for private schools or schools in other LEAs?* Clare Market Papers No.1. London: Centre for Educational Research, London School of Economics.

West, A., Varlaam, A. & Scott, G. (1991) Choice of high school: pupils' perceptions, *Educational Research*, 33, pp. 207-215.

Whitty, G., Edwards, T. & Fitz, J. (1989) England and Wales: the role of the private sector, in G. Walford (Ed.) *Private Schools in Ten Countries: policy and practice.* London: Routledge.

Woods, P. (1992) Empowerment through choice? Towards an understanding of parental choice and school responsiveness, *Educational Management and Administration*, 20, pp. 204-211.

Oxford Studies in Comparative Education, Vol. 6(1), 1996

Market Trends in the French School System: overt policy, hidden strategies, actual changes

AGNÈS VAN ZANTEN

Like many other school systems around the world, French schools have undergone significant transformations in the 1980s and 1990s that are related to the progressive introduction of market trends. A complex interplay of government policy, consumers' demands, organizational arrangements and school agents' practices has led to an increase in the diversity of provision and an extension of parental choice of school. Using the available results from interesting but still very scarce statistical studies and qualitative research reports on this topic, this paper presents an overview of observed changes and explores some of their potential consequences.

Organizational Changes, Consumers' Demands and Government Policy

Despite centralization and standardization of state education, diversity of provision has long been a structural component of the French school system owing to the existence of an important private sector, mostly of catholic affiliation. The relationship between the state and the public schools on one side and the catholic authorities and private schools on the other has been both one of intense ideological conflict and of complex organizational arrangements that have led to the present State subsidized private sector which receives 15 per cent of the total school population. The special status of private schools requires that they offer the same national curriculum as public schools and that they accept pupils of all confessions, but it leaves them free to promote a specific school ethos and educational style and to receive pupils from anywhere in the country. More important for the subject under discussion here is that, although some secularized versions of the religious ideal still remain in these educational styles and ethos, private schools comprise today a diversity of institutions that, playing down their

63

religious identity, tend to promote themselves as a resort for dissatisfied clients of the public sector. Some promote academic excellence, others 'sell' their disciplinarian methods, still others specialize in remedial teaching (Ballion, 1982; Bonvin, 1982).

Evidence that parents make abundant use of this diversity of provision is seen in the importance of 'sector-switching' (if the number of pupils who have ever attended the private sector is taken into account, the 15 per cent proportion rises to almost one-third of the school population). But of particular importance is that this 'sector-switching' often takes place at crucial moments of choice among several academic routes and especially if parents and adolescents disagree with proposals made to them within the public sector (Langouèt & Léger, 1991). Unconscious of (or unwilling to acknowledge) these changes in school provision and parental demand, in 1984 the Socialist government tried to reduce State subsidies to the private sector as a first move towards abolition of the specific status of private schools. It was confronted, however, with a huge demonstration of parents from the private – but also to some extent from the public – sector who stood up in defence of 'freedom of choice' and forced the government to backtrack and to accept the *status quo*. Diversity of provision and parental choice in the public sector have been considerably affected by the public-private debate. Private school policies and parental strategies of 'sector-switching' revealed that the public schools were perceived less as democratic institutions than as institutions that imposed a series of constraints on parents' rights in education.

In order to understand changes inside the public sector, it is also important to point out the tensions created by the move towards unification and democratization of the school system that started after World War One but became effective, following important structural reforms, in the 1960s and 1970s. During the 19th century, the French system was characterized by a strong division between elite classic education which took place in the *lycées* (these were secondary level institutions but also included at that time the 'petites classes de lycée' which gave elementary education) and popular education which took place in elementary schools. A third sector also existed that comprised various kinds of secondary modern and technical education and attracted boys and girls from the independent middle-classes. These three sectors were progressively integrated into a common system by various reforms that created the *collège unique*, which was roughly the equivalent of comprehensive secondary schools in Britain.

These reforms produced major changes in school recruitment as new secondary schools were created, tracks and options redistributed and catchment areas firmly demarcated through the procedure known as the *carte scolaire* (school chart) whose declared aims were to rationalize pupils' flow and orientation within the school system but also to reduce geographical inequalities in access to schooling. These reforms also brought about major changes in the schools' internal functioning as teaching and disciplinarian techniques had to be adapted to the new pupil intake and new goals of democratization. As a result of this, they generated intense frustration among teachers and other school personnel who felt that their professional identity was being threatened, and among middle class parents who felt that homogenization was levelling down school results. This explains why, in the 1970s and early 1980s, a growing number of school agents and parents started to develop various strategies to turn around procedures of recruitment and of internal allocation of pupils into classes imposed by educational authorities.

Forced to take these various elements into account, the Socialist government started to experiment in 1984 with a policy of limited choice called *decentralization* which consisted in allowing parents in some areas to select one of five different *collèges* within the official limits set by local commissions on the number of pupils per class and per school. This procedure was extended to other areas by the new right-wing government elected in 1986. This government counted among its political supporters (but not as one of its most influential figures) the author of a book called *To liberate the school: schooling 'à la carte'* (Madelin, 1984) who represented the most liberal fraction of the UDF (Union pour la Démocratie Française) party. *Decentralization* was broadened to include the *lycées* in 1988. It applies today to about half of all secondary schools in France, although precise figures are not available at the Ministry of Education. Other measures such as the redefinition of catchment areas so that, theoretically, more parents can have access to prestigious public schools or the enlargement of catchment areas to include more internal diversity of provision, have also been taken by some local educational administrations, especially in big cities.

Diversity of provision has also been enlarged by various measures related to decentralization of educational control. One distinctive feature of the French educational system has been the concentration at the State level of decision-making powers concerning almost every aspect of instruction: examinations, curriculum, teacher recruitment and careers and system evaluation. It is important to note, however, that although some researchers have tended to conceive of this as a structural characteristic of French organizations (Crozier & Friedberg, 1977), the centralization and standardization of educational provision is a complex historical process that has served various, and sometimes contradictory, ends. More important to our purpose here is that, for a long period, centralization was not incompatible with the existence of a plurality of educational institutions which at the local level frequently competed with each other for pupils and resources (Briand & Chapoulie, 1993). It is also important not to confuse locus and strength of control. As Broadfoot (1985) has pointed out, bureaucracies such as the French school system allow considerable room for teachers' individual autonomy.

It is only since the upheaval created by the reforms presented above that the centralized system began to be strongly criticized. As a response to these criticisms and also as a way of gaining financial support from regional bodies and local communities, the Socialist government promulgated in 1982 and 1985, as part of a global decentralization reform, a law on decentralization of education, which gave to each administrative level (Regions, Departments and Municipalities) new competence for each educational level. Regions became responsible for *lycées* and professional education, Departments for *collèges*, and Municipalities for infant and primary schools. This law also gave more financial autonomy to secondary schools. In addition to this, in 1989, the *Loi d'Orientation*, extended to primary schools and *lycées* the obligation, first experimented in *collèges*, to develop a three-year specific project that should be evaluated every year by local educational administrators and could serve to obtain extra resources for specific actions from local educational administrations, local political authorities or independent firms. This law also gave more power to parents in decisions concerning choice of track or type of school and the possibility of opposing teachers' proposals for grade repeating.

Parental Choice of School: maximizing benefits, fostering specific forms of socialization

In order to understand French parents' opinions and practices concerning school choice, some elements concerning the general evolution of parental ideologies and practices concerning schooling must be pointed out. As concerns ideologies, in spite of the reduction of professional benefits received from the possession of educational credentials and of the growth of youth unemployment even among qualified youngsters, the majority of parents still believe that there is a strong relationship between educational attainment and occupational status. As a consequence, parents of all social categories tend to have high expectations concerning their children's school careers. A recent statistical study conducted by the evaluation department of the Ministry of Education shows for instance that 76 per cent of parents hope that their children will continue their studies up to the age of 20 and beyond, while 50 per cent think that a higher education degree is the most useful certification to get a job (Caille, 1992). And in practice, the number of pupils who obtain the baccalauréat has exploded (9.7 per cent of a generation in 1959, 23.7 per cent in 1974, and more than 50 per cent today), as well as that of university students. In the terms of Passeron (1982), parents' expectations and efforts to keep their children at school can be interpreted as a strategy to maximize educational capital in a period where the social return of this investment has a tendency to decrease.

Another important dimension of French parents' ideologies on schooling is the central role historically attributed to the public or common school as the main instrument of social integration, of the political construction of citizenship and of the rational transmission of a universal culture. This 19th century ideal model has come under attack both from the majority who feel that it must be maintained but in a renewed form and from the minority who feel that it is no longer applicable to 20th century French urban, mobile, multi-ethnic society. Nevertheless, it still plays a central ideological function in preventing parents who send their children to the public sector from publicly pleading for or acknowledging the existence of specific forms of socialization in each school. However, in practice, the progressive dilution of institutional aims opens a new space for parental strategies of social distinction in school (Bourdieu, 1979). As in Britain, the search for social segregation becomes an important dimension of parental efforts to try to control the effects of teachers and classmates on values and behaviours associated with specific class positions (Ball et al, 1994; van Zanten, 1996a).

A third important factor that plays an important role in parents' ideologies and practices today is the model of the 'professional parent'. Although strongly associated with middle-class women's investment in education, this model is largely diffused by the press and other mass media. Most parents are now convinced that the transmission of an initial cultural capital is not enough and that they must keep informed, help their children daily and carefully negotiate decisions concerning choice of tracks and schools with them and with school personnel (van Zanten, 1996b). Although there might be a significant gap between discourse and practice, it is important to note that a recent national study on the educational efforts of parents (Gissot et al, 1994) shows that parents of all categories admit to spending considerable time and money in helping children with homework, providing educational resources and educational activities at home or in specialized centres and meeting teachers and school personnel. On the other hand, in comparison with other countries, French parents have never had an important role to play in the everyday functioning of schools. They were considered as subjects of a state system of education whose main responsibility was vis-à-vis pupils, the would-be citizens. Recent reforms have greatly increased parents' individual influence on their children's school careers rather than encouraged their collective participation in school decisions and activities.

How does choice intervene in this specific configuration? In fact, research conducted in 1986, two years after the experimental procedure of *desectorization* took place, showed that only 10 per cent of families in a sample of 22,000 pupils and 149 *collèges* effectively used their right to choose among five different schools proposed by local educational administrations. National statistics on authorized choice today at the *collège* or the *lycée* level are not available but local figures do not show a significant increase of this proportion. However, choice also operates at another official level through dispensations granted to parents from local pupil allocation rules. Accepted motives for exceptions are: choice of an option (especially a language option) that does not exist in the district school, desire to send the child to a school near the parents' workplace and not necessarily near their home, presence of another member of the family in the desired school. In addition to this, it is important to mention choice strategies that rely on 'illegal' means to get satisfaction such as giving as one's personal address that of a relative, a friend or even an outside person willing to 'sell' his geographical location in the recruitment area of the desired *collège* or *lycée*, or negotiating privately with headteachers without informing the school authorities. Statistics on these practices are rarely available, for understandable reasons. A recent study conducted by the evaluation department of the Ministry of Education shows, however, that this still remains a relatively marginal phenomenon: in a national sample of 27,000 pupils in their first year of secondary education only 10 per cent went to public schools other than their 'sector' school and 18 per cent went to private schools (Caille, 1993).

Although choice remains relatively modest in proportion to other countries, it still shows considerable variation across social classes. Parents from the bourgeoisie have traditionally send their children either to private schools who recruit pupils from a large geographical area, even at a national or international level, or to public or private schools located near their place of residence. Given the concentration of parents belonging to this social class in prestigious city centres or selected urban social districts where the best *lycées* are generally located, 'selection by mortgage' has guaranteed in most cases both good – although not necessarily excellent – instructional quality and social segregation. As for primary education, a recent sociological study conducted in one of the affluent districts of Paris shows that, when these parents do not choose the private sector either for convenience or for ideological reasons, they act in such a way as to 'privatize' the public school where they are both numerically and socially in a dominant position: they use their political and social relations to better physical facilities, obtain educational materials of the highest quality and increase the number of outside activities. They exert considerable influence on the choice of textbooks and teaching methods and insist on frequent evaluation of pupils' results. (Pinçon & Pinçon-Charlot, 1989). For these parents, new possibilities for choice do not appear necessary. On the contrary, they may become threatening if high proportions of middle-class and lower-class parents had access to some of the schools they presently control.

The majority of working-class and, to an even greater extent, immigrant parents, on the other hand, send their children to public schools. Given the increase of social and ethnic segregation in big cities, many of these children have a great probability of attending segregated schools, characterized by a high degree of teacher mobility, few attractive options and low achievement levels. It is therefore not surprising to observe than in these deprived areas French parents who have better jobs, higher levels of education and children with better school results than the majority of other families, tend to avoid the local school to a significant extent (Léger & Tripier, 1986). It is not certain, however, than these parents really make rational choices, as it appears in many cases that parents react more in a subjective way to what they perceive as the bad reputation of the local school, than make informed choices of other schools (Henriot-van Zanten, 1990). In addition to this, it is important to note that these practices concern only a minority of working-class parents. Most of them, as shown in the *desectorization* survey mentioned above, do not make choices even when invited to do so because of lack of information on the new procedures or on the schools themselves, which are frequently seen as roughly equivalent. When they do choose, actual choices tend to be guided by financial and convenience considerations – distance, means of transportation – or by a perception of school provision or climate that is not directed towards the search for excellence or strict discipline but rather towards the search for social compatibility with their own cultural interests and norms – options in technology or professional subjects or for some immigrant parents, in their mother language, or a 'warm' atmosphere (Ballion, 1986).

Middle-class parents seem to profit more from *desectorization*, in the same way that before and even now it is middle-class parents who make more use of the various legal and illegal means to have access to desired *collèges* and *lycées*. This is especially the case for the intellectual upper and middle-grade executives and for professionals or semi-professionals working in the public sector. They generally have more credentials and higher educational aspirations than middle-class parents working in the private sector or than independent workers, but have neither the financial resources which will allow them to have access to expensive private schools or to move to the more residential areas where prestigious public schools are located, nor in some cases the desire to send their children to local private schools (Pinçon-Charlot & Rendu, 1988). Parents who are teachers, especially those who teach at the secondary level, appear in the survey on *desectorization* as the social category the most inclined to choose within the public sector and to so do in putting down as first factors for choice those traditionally associated with excellence: very high achievement levels, location in the city centre, more than 20 per cent of pupils coming from the upper class. This shows both the complex way in which families from these social milieux try to reconcile their attachment to the public sector with their high academic ambitions for their children, and the importance of being an 'insider' able to decode and manipulate the complex functioning of the system (Ball et al, 1995).

School Policies and Headteachers' Recruitment Strategies: maintaining achievement levels, creating new images

To understand parental strategies it is nevertheless necessary to consider simultaneously the changes that have been taking place in schools, especially in secondary schools. An important element to take into account concerns the previous effects of the ideology of the common school, of the standardized and centralized mode of allocation of resources and of the strict delimitation of catchment areas on diversity of provision. On the one hand, these factors have contributed to maintain a variation in achievement levels among schools much lower in France than in countries such as the Netherlands, Germany, Switzerland or the United States. On the other hand, they have brought about increasing variation among pupils within the same school, which remains higher than in many other OECD countries (OECD, 1991, 1994). One of the main reasons for this is that since the 1970s headteachers and teachers have tried to cope with the administrative, pedagogical and discipline problems created by the massive inflow of pupils from working-class and immigrants families not so much by selection procedures at entry – although these exist in certain schools – but by the internal distribution of pupils into different tracks or ability-level groups either with the agreement of the local educational authorities or in more clandestine ways. This seems an upward trend at the moment as it is more and more demanded by parents who are unable or unwilling to make the choice of a school other than the 'sector' one.

This trend, however, takes different forms in different types of schools. The old, well-established *lycées* have maintained their reputation through provision of prestigious tracks and particularly of *Classes préparatoires aux Grandes Ecoles*, that is, higher education sections that prepare for entrance into the highly selective *Grandes Ecoles* which train the French intellectual and managerial elite, and through excellent results in the *baccalauréat*. They also provide, in subtle ways, specific forms of socialization by means of academic traditions, choice of specific sections (humanities, sciences, commercial or technical) and selection of teachers and pupils. These *lycées*, which are frequently located in the centre of big cities and are in most cases over-subscribed, have always been able, with the official or the unofficial consent of local educational administrations, to select their pupils and have been up to now very little affected by changes in state goals and in the social and ethnic composition of secondary schools' population. Nevertheless, in order to maintain their achievement level and continue to be able to select the very best among prospective pupils, these schools work hard to keep their good results in the *baccalauréat* – and thus exclude from some tracks or from the school altogether those pupils who do less well – and compete with each other to maintain their prestigious tracks and options or create new ones.

Other *lycées* and *collèges* which are not so renowned and are located in socially mixed areas are necessarily more subject to parental pressures. Principals and teachers who want to maintain the reputation of their school and to continue to attract French, middle-class pupils and high achievers tend to respond, and more and more frequently to anticipate, implicit or explicit parental demands for internal differentiation by the setting-up of classes subtly differentiated by their social, sexual and ethnic structure and by pupils' level of achievement. This internal hierarchy may be signalled by the presence of prestigious options ('exotic' languages such as Chinese or Russian, dead languages such as Latin and Greek, European sections which combine two languages) that have to be obtained from local educational administrators and are thus a source of intensive competition among schools located in the same area. Frequently, however, the hierarchy is 'home-made', that is headteachers and teachers set up classes such as 'theatre' 'special mathematics' or 'reinforced language' whose real significance – that may vary considerably from one school to another – is only perceived by those parents who are able to decode subtle messages about the level, the general atmosphere or the social and ethnic intake of each (Payet, 1995).

Some *collèges* and *lycées* located in very deprived areas have little or no organizational strategies geared towards the retention or the attraction of 'good' students, other than trying to keep in touch with their feeder schools to reinforce institutional links (Woods et al, 1994). A fraction of these schools, more frequently those that have been part for several years of educational priority zones – that is, deprived areas where, like in British EPAs, schools have benefited from a positive discrimination treatment to set up specific projects adapted to their problems – have developed opposite policies. They have voluntarily or involuntarily adapted teachers' expectations, curriculum and teaching methods to the perceived needs and wants of disadvantaged populations. Nevertheless, falling demographic rates, housing policies and the increase in the number of parents who seek to avoid these schools do create a survival problem for certain schools of this kind. It is therefore not surprising that many of them try to develop at least one attractive option to maintain their intake level. With the agreement in many cases of local school authorities, such options are felt to be necessary to partially redress the degraded image of these schools and to reduce or at least contain social and ethnic school segregation.

These practices suppose that important changes have taken place in the ethical principles and professional ideologies of school agents. In fact, there is a large consensus among researchers that teachers have been particularly affected by the scale and the succession of reforms since the 1970s. Some sociologists point out that these reforms have led to a growing dissociation between professional status – that is from the professional ethos shaped by training, previous practice and the ideological positions of unions and professional associations, as well as by state policy and specific organizational regulations – and required skills in everyday activity (Dubet, 1991). Other authors insist that these changes have led school agents to disenchantment and thus to cynical, individualistic positions or to the search for local arrangements that maintain peace and the everyday activity of schools, but do not bother with consequences at the global level (Derouet, 1988, 1992). My own research shows that most teachers accept the development of an educational quasi-market in France as an inevitable phenomenon. Although they frequently express disagreement with government and school policies for diversification and with parental consumerist attitudes, they think that there is little they can do in this respect and leave the responsibility for developing new formal and informal forms of market regulation to local educational administrators and headteachers. This is the case even for those teachers who are particularly active in their classrooms or who are involved in collective educational projects (van Zanten, 1996c).

This points to another phenomenon that has been observed in recent field studies and that has recently been explored in a quantitative survey conducted by the Ministry of Education – that is the growing distance between the ideologies and professional practices of headteachers and teachers (Guillaume & Maresca, 1993). In the past, headteachers were certainly not educational leaders in the British sense. They were mostly administrators with little autonomy who guaranteed the application of state and local policies in the schools. Nevertheless, as they were trained as teachers and had frequently taught for some years before becoming headteachers, they remained close to the concerns of the teacher body. Today, having gained more autonomy and more responsibility concerning the everyday running of schools, headteachers are much more likely to be attentive to problems of financial management. They spend considerable time in activities such as promoting the school or negotiating new resources with educational and political authorities. A fraction of them even see their work as more close to that of business managers than to that of teachers. It is important to note that these changes have been accompanied by changes in their recruitment and training that set them apart from teachers.

These practices have also been reinforced by decentralization in several ways. First, by giving more autonomy to secondary schools and by making it compulsory for each *école*, *collège* or *lycée* to develop its own project, the government has encouraged diversity within the system. This diversity, however, remains much more centred on the quality of instructional provision than on specific school ethos. Secondly, diversity of provision is also being fostered by the increasing involvement of local political bodies in education. These elected officials want efficacy, quick results and also some schools to become 'shopwindows' of their recent investments in education. They thus tend to reward traditional well-established schools that are part of the brand image of the city or old and new schools that play the market to improve their image. They can do this in several ways: by contributing to the betterment of physical facilities, by financing educational projects, trips and promotional activities such as the edition of brochures or the organization of school open days and, even in some cases by contributing to the in-service training of headteachers in managerial and evaluation techniques (Henriot-van Zanten, 1993).

Conclusion: social and academic effects of the introduction of market principles in education

Although the French educational system has formally introduced only limited diversity and choice and although educational authorities, teachers and parents alike are reluctant to publicly acknowledge the existence of various kinds of hidden strategies that work in that sense, it is clear that the ideal of the common school and of equality of opportunity for all citizens is being replaced by the ideal of the 'patterned' school geared towards the satisfaction of specific customers (Lareau, 1990; Ball, 1992). The class and ethnic bias of the first model have been clearly shown by various sociological works (Bourdieu & Passeron, 1970; Baudelot & Establet, 1971; Berthelot, 1983) and it is certainly impossible to try make it work today without thinking of new ways of integrating differentiation and choice. However, the consequences of an extensive application of the second model must be explored in detail to see how well it fares as a real alternative.

As can be deduced from the above, one of the most immediate effects of the introduction of a limited dose of market ideology in French education could be a progressive destruction of school agents' work ethics. To a certain extent, this destruction could be salutary in the sense of forcing school agents to reconsider the limits of the common school's model and to be more aware of their own role in maintaining or reducing differences between social groups. However, the shock provoked by this destruction will certainly lead teachers to assume defensive positions more than it will lead to the development of renewed contextualized work ethics. In addition to this, it could lead some teachers and especially headteachers, as is already the case in Britain (Ball et al, 1993), to gear their professional practice to a universe of competition and impression management that carries them away from pedagogical concerns.

Another even more important effect of the introduction of market ideology in French education could be the increase of segregation according to social and ethnic origin. Similarly to what happens in Britain (Bagley, 1995), parents who choose rarely mention the social or ethnic composition of the school explicitly, but attributes such as 'good reputation' or 'quality of the neighbourhood' that can be taken at least in part as proxies for the first are mentioned by more than half of them (respectively 62.5 per cent and 51.6 per cent) to qualify the *lycée* requested as first choice. In addition to this, it is important to note that while high proportions of parents declare themselves to be ill-informed about teachers' dynamism (50.3 per cent) or competence (33.4 per cent) or about the quality of the relationship between teachers and pupils (45.6 per cent), most of them feel that they have enough elements to perceive qualities associated with the social and ethnic intake of the school (Ballion, 1991). As parents who can choose and have the wish to do so are more likely to belong to the French middle class or upper working class, lower-class and immigrant parents become victims of choice not only because avoided schools become highly segregated but because pupils who leave are not only white and middle-class but 'good' pupils and thus their departure reinforces the idea that it is the presence of poor and immigrant children that lowers academic standards (Léger & Tripier, 1986).

The relationship between social and ethnic segregation and pupils' achievement and school careers is certainly not a simple one. Nevertheless, the results of research in several countries indicate that lower-class children tend to express higher educational ambitions and make more progress in mixed or middle-class schools than in lower-class schools. This is so both because of the leading effect of other pupils and families and also because teachers tend to adjust their expectations, syllabuses, teaching methods and evaluation criteria to social context (Duru-Bellat & Henriot-van Zanten, 1992). In addition to this, recent French research also suggests that there is a link between the development of segregation between schools and between classes inside schools and the increase in pupils' violence. Pupils seem to feel strongly stigmatised and excluded by these practices that introduce subtle hierarchies and inequalities in a system that pretends to be democratic and integrative. If this is so, then the introduction of market principles in education will reinforce both social inequality and social disintegration and exclusion.

References

Ball, S.J. (1982) Education markets, choice and social class: the market as a class strategy in the UK and the USA, *British Journal of Sociology of Education*, 14, pp. 3-19.

Ball, S.J., Bowe, R. & Gewirtz, S. (1993) Competitive schooling: values, ethics and cultural engineering, paper presented at the American Educational Research Association annual meeting, Atlanta.

Ball, S.J., Gewirtz, S. & Bowe, R. (1994) School choice, social class and distinction: the realisation of social advantage in education. London: Centre for Educational Studies.

Ball, S.J., Bowe, R. & Gewirtz, S. (1995) Circuits of schooling: a sociological exploration of parental choice in social class contexts, *Sociological Review*, 43, pp. 52-78.

Ballion, R. (1982) *Les consommateurs d'école.* Paris: Stock.

Ballion, R. (1986) Le choix du collège: le comportement 'éclairé' des familles, *Revue Française de Sociologie*, 27, pp. 719-734.

Ballion, R. (1991) *La bonne école.* Paris: Hatier.

Baudelot, C. & Establet, R. (1971) *L'école Capitaliste en France.* Pa:is, Maspéro.

Berthelot, J.M. (1983) *Le Piège Scolaire.* Paris: PUF.

Bonvin, F. (1982) L'école catholique est-elle encore religieuse?, *Actes de la Recherche en Sciences Sociales*, 44-45, pp. 95-108.

Bourdieu, P. (1979) *La Distinction: critique sociale du jugement.* Paris: Minuit.

Bourdieu, P. & Passeron, J.C. (1970) *La Reproduction: eléments pour une théorie du système d'enseignement.* Paris: Minuit.

Briand, J.P. & Chapoulie, J.M. (1993) L'institution scolaire et la scolarisation : une perspective d'ensemble, *Revue Française de Sociologie*, 34, pp. 3-42.

Broadfoot, P. (1985) Towards conformity: educational control and the growth of corporate management in England and France, in J. Lauglo, M. McLean (Eds.) *The Control of Education: international perspectives on the centralization-decentralization debate.* London: Heinemann.

Caille, J.P. (1992), Les parents d'élève de collège et les études de leur enfant: attentes et degré d'implication, *Education et Formations*, 32.

Caille, J.P. (1993) Le choix d'un collège public situé en dehors du secteur de domiciliation, *Note d'information*, 93-19, D.E.P.

Crozier, M. & Friedberg, E. (1977) *L'acteur et le Système*. Paris: Seuil.

Derouet, J.L. (1988) Désaccords et arrangements dans les collèges (1981-1986), *Revue Française de Pédagogie*, 83, pp. 5-22.

Derouet, J.L. (1992) *Ecole et Justice: de l'égalité des chances aux compromis locaux*. Paris: A.M. Métailié.

Dubet, F. (1991) *Les Lycéens*. Paris: Seuil.

Durubellat, M. & Henriot-van Zanten, A. (1992) *Sociologie de l'école*. Paris: A. Colin.

Gissot, C., Heran, F. & Manon, N. (1994) *Les Efforts Éducatifs des Familles*. Paris: INSEE, coll. INSEE Résultats.

Guillaume, F.R. & Maresca, B. (1993) Les chefs d'établissement et l'autonomie, *Education et Formations*, 35, pp. 43-51.

Henriot-van Zanten, A. (1990) *L'école et l'espace local*. Lyon: Presses Universitaires de Lyon.

Henriot-van Zanten, A. (1993) Les politiques éducatives locales entre l'Etat et le marché, *Société Française*, 48, pp. 4-10.

Langouët, G. & Léger, A. (1991) *Public ou privé? Trajectoires et réussites scolaires*. Paris: Publidix/Editions de l'espace Européen.

Lareau, A. (1990) *Home Advantage*. New York: Falmer.

Léger, A. & Tripier, M. (1986) *Fuir ou Construire l'école Populaire?* Paris: MéridiensKlincksieck.

Madelin, A. (1984) *Pour libérer l'école, l'enseignement à la Carte*. Paris: Robert Laffont.

OCDE (1990) *L'enseignement dans les pays de l'OCDE*. Paris: OCDE.

OCDE (1994) *Le choix de l'école*. Paris: OCDE.

Passeron, J.C. (1982) L'inflation des diplômes. Remarques sur l'usage de quelques concepts analogiques en sociologie, *Revue Française de Sociologie*, 23, pp. 551-584.

Payet, J.P. (1995) *Collèges de Banlieue*. Paris: Méridiensklincksieck

Pinçon, M. & Pinçon-Charlot, M. (1989) *Dans les Beaux Quartiers*. Paris: Seuil.

Pinçon-Charlot, M. & Rendu, P. (1988) Les hauts fonctionnaires face aux enjeux scolaires de leurs enfants, *Revue Française de Pédagogie*, 83, pp. 51-56.

Van Zanten, A. (1996a) Fabrication et effets de la ségrégation scolaire, in S. Paugam (Ed.) *L'exclusion: l'état des savoirs*. Paris: La Découverte.

Van Zanten, A. (1996b) Stratégies utilitaristes et stratégies identitaires des parents vis-à-vis de l'école: une relecture critique des analyses sociologiques, *Lien Social et Politiques* (in press).

Van Zanten, A. (1996c) Les transformations des pratiques et des éthiques professionnelles dans les établissements, in R. Bourdoncle & L. Demailly (Eds.) *Les professions de l'éducation*. Bruxelles: De Boeck (in press).

Woods, P., Bagley, C. & Glatter, R. (1994) Dynamics of competition: the effects of local competitive arenas on schools, paper presented at CEDAR International Conference 'Changing Educational Structures: policy and practice', University of Warwick, 15-17 April.

Oxford Studies in Comparative Education, Vol. 6(1), 1996

Germany: competitive inequality in educational quasi-markets

MANFRED WEISS & BRIGITTE STEINERT

Characterisation of 'Quasi-markets' in the German School System

Supply-side: the macro-structure of secondary schooling

A distinctive feature of the German educational system is the differentiated and hierarchically organized (basic) structure of secondary education with three school types: the Hauptschule (short-course secondary school, grades 5-9 or 10), the Realschule (intermediate school, grades 5-10), and the selective Gymnasium (grammar school, grades 5-12 in East Germany, grades 5-13 in West Germany). Some Länder have introduced the Gesamtschule (comprehensive school) which integrates or combines the three different types of secondary schools as an alternative or sometimes as a substitute alongside the traditional schools. With unification in 1990 the reconstituted Länder of East Germany have adopted a school structure similar to that of the West German Länder. With the exception of Mecklenburg-West Pomerania, the East German Länder have, however, refrained from establishing the Hauptschule, responding to the rapidly decreasing attractiveness of this school type experienced by the 'old' Länder (see below). Alongside the Gymnasium there is a differently labelled type of general secondary school at the lower secondary level that combines Hauptschule and Realschule courses (Führ, 1992; Rolff, 1994a). After four (in Brandenburg and Berlin six) years of primary schooling at a uniform Grundschule all children transfer to one of these types of secondary schools, according to their ability (achievement level at primary school) and their parents' preferences.

The organisation of upper-secondary general education in Eastern and Western Germany follows the concept of the Reformed Gymnasium Upper Level which offers a broad spectrum of compulsory and optional courses as well as different course levels (basic, advanced), enabling the individualisation of a pupil's programme of study through choice. In contrast to the West German pattern the Länder in East Germany (except Brandenburg) decided on a 2-year course at upper-secondary level (grades 11 and 12) instead of the 3-year course at West German schools (grades 11-13), i.e. the Abitur that qualifies for general university entrance can already be obtained after 12 years of schooling. Organizationally the upper-secondary level usually is part of a Gymnasium, it can, however, also be affiliated to a comprehensive school or exist as a separate school unit.

The diversity of the German general education system does not manifest itself fully in the formally differentiated school structure. Differentiations of curricular and extracurricular profiles can also occur especially within the group of Gymnasien (emphasising e.g. classical languages, modern languages or mathematics/natural sciences). Private schools – mainly denominational schools, but also Rudolf Steiner schools, free schools, and recently international schools – complete the school provision. The pluralistic supply structure seems 'postmodern' in character. It is, however, also an indication of the impossibility of reaching consensus on a uniform school structure. From an economic point of view the highly differentiated German school system can be regarded as quite an expensive means of preserving 'peace in school policy'.

Parents and pupils formally have the right to choose among the diverse number of types of schools or school careers as laid down in the constitution or school law of a Land. This right can, however, only be exercised if a sufficient variety of options is actually available within reasonable proximity to their homes. For political, demographic and economic reasons this is quite often not the case in reality (see below). Frequently parents have to rely on the school provision outside their residential area and sometimes in adjoining communities to realise the preferred choice of secondary school (contrary to the primary school sector, in secondary education with the partial exception of Hauptschulen no fixed catchment areas exist). Non-residential pupils can, however, be rejected if the preferred school operates at full capacity. Choosing a school outside the residential area implies in many cases that 'transaction costs' accrue to families in the form of time and expenses of transportation (usually transportation costs will not be refunded by the state or community if an equivalent alternative to the chosen school is available nearer home).

Configurations of School Provision at the Micro-level:
qualification of 'educational quasi-markets'

The diversity of school provision varies considerably between communities and between districts. Following Bargel & Kuthe (1992), five different configurations can be identified at community level:
1. communities without any secondary school or with only one short-course secondary school;

2. communities with an incompletely structured school system: short-course secondary and intermediate school or short-course secondary school and Gymnasium;
3. communities with a completely structured school system: short-course secondary school, intermediate school, Gymnasium;
4. communities with an integrated system: comprehensive school, and in parts remnants of the structured school system;
5. communities with a diverse school environment: all four types of schools are available – often several times (partly with different profiles) and frequently supplemented by private schools.

The first two configurations represent the typical pattern found in many small communities in rural areas. The third and fourth configurations at least provide the full range of possible school-leaving certificates. The term 'educational quasi-market' applies only to the fifth configuration, characterising a competitive school environmen, in which differentiated educational demands can be met. This situation is mainly found in cities and conurbations.

Regional disparities in school provision are the result not only of differences in population density, size and the economic and social structure of communities and districts, but also of differences in educational policy. The overall effect of these factors on school provision becomes evident when comparing, for example, the situation in Baden-Württemberg, a Land governed by the conservative party for a long time which preferred the tripartite school system, and North Rhine-Westphalia, a Land with a social democratic government (until recently) that preferred integrated school structures. Whereas in Baden-Württemberg nearly 28 per cent of all communities provided no secondary schooling at all and nearly 40 per cent provided the short-course secondary school as the only type of secondary schooling in 1990/91, the respective percentages for North Rhine-Westphalia are 1.3 and 20.2. The figures show furthermore that in Baden-Württemberg almost 16 per cent of the communities offer the whole range of school-leaving certificates as against 42 per cent of the communities in North Rhine-Westphalia. A diverse school supply, being constitutive of an educational quasi-market, is available in only 2.5 per cent of the communities in Baden-Württemberg, but in nearly 17 per cent of the communities in North Rhine-Westphalia (compare Bargel & Kuthe, 1992, p. 47).

Demand-side: aspirations, educational participation and
formal school qualification

The decisive choice in children's school careers is made at the transition from primary school to secondary education. Within the formal school structure school choice is highly influenced by the school-leaving certificates that can be obtained in the different school types, as they are of outstanding importance in allocating occupational and societal positions. Table 1 shows the findings of surveys, conducted regularly since 1979, on parents' educational aspirations regarding their children's school-leaving certificates (Rolff et al, 1994b, p. 16).

	Short-course secondary school-leaving certificate (Hauptschule)	Intermediate school-leaving certificate (Realschule)	Qualification for university entrance (Abitur)	
	%	%	%	N
West Germany				
1,979	31*	32	37	1,143
1,981	17	38	45	890
1,983	13	36	51	765
1,985	11	35	54	726
1,987	11	37	52	735
1,989	10	34	56	706
1,991	11	36	53	704
1,993	13	39	48	749
East Germany				
1991	13	36	51	550
1,993	13	42	45	494
Germany, total				
1,991	12	36	52	1,177
1,993	13	39	48	1,261

Table I. What kind of final school-leaving certificate would you like your child to obtain. *In the 1979 survey the answer "completion of Hauptschule" comprises an apprenticeship certificate. Source: Rolff et al, 1994b, p. 16.

The percentages in Table I show that the proportion of parents who are content with a Hauptschule-certificate for their children as final school-leaving qualification decreased significantly from 31 per cent in 1979 to 10 per cent in 1989. At the same time the proportion of parents who want their children to attain the highest school-leaving certificate, the Abitur (which is the qualification necessary for general university entrance), increased from 37 per cent to a peak of 56 per cent. This trend reflects two developments: a rise in the parents' own educational level during the period of educational expansion in the 1960s and 1970s ('echo-effect') and the developments: a rise in the parents' own educational level during the period of educational expansion in the 1960s and 1970s ('echo-effect') and the increase in vocational and societal requirements making the Abitur a necessary qualification for an ever growing number of occupations.

Since 1989 the expressed preference for the Abitur has declined in favour of a 'middle qualification' (Realschule-certificate or an equivalent qualification), indicating, on the one hand, a possible temporary 'saturation effect' and, on the other hand, the deteriorated conditions in the labour market for university graduates as well as the overloaded state at institutions of higher education, which made vocational training increasingly attractive and caused parents, especially with lower-class social backgrounds to adapt their aspirations downwards. Nevertheless, a total of nearly 90 per cent of the parents in East and West Germany at least strive for a 'middle qualification', now considered the minimum standard.

The comparison between parents' aspirations and actual educational participation (Table II) clearly shows that it is a difference between wishes and reality. The obvious mismatch is the result of limitations on the supply-side (lack of school provision within reasonable distance of home) as well as selection and self-selection mechanisms (school entrance examination or trial period of instruction if the aspirations of parents exceed the primary school teacher's recommendation, to avoid the risk of school failure). There is sufficient empirical evidence to conclude that both factors work to the disadvantage of the lower social classes.

School type	1960 %	1970 %	1980 %	1990 %	1993* %
Short-course secondary school (Hauptschule)	63.9	55.4	40.3	34.2	25.6
Integrated classes for short-course secondary school and intermediate school (Haupt- und Realschule)	–	–	–	–	7.4
Intermediate school (Realschule)	15.6	21.5	28.2	28.8	26.1
Grammar School (Gymnasium)	20.5	23.1	27.5	30.8	31.4
Integrated comprehensive school (Integrierie Gesamtschule)	–	–	4.0	6.2	8.9

Table II. Proportion of pupils in grades 7-9 attending different types of school. 1960-1990 the former Federal Republic of Germany only. Source: Der Bundesminister für Bildung und Wissenschaft (Ed.) Grund- und Strukturdaten, 1992-1993, p. 66. *1993: Germany, now including East Germany. The percentages refer to pupils attending grade 8 only. Source: Ständige Konferenz der Kultusminister der Länder in der Bundesrepublik Deutschland (Ed.) 1994, p. viii and p. xix.

As indicated in Table II the share of pupils attending short-course secondary schools (Hauptschulen) has decreased considerably, whereas the enrolment rates at school types which confer the highest school-leaving certificate (Gymnasien and comprehensive schools with Gymnasium upper level) increased steadily. The percentages from the 1980s onwards show a relatively stable picture for intermediate schools (Realschulen). The figures on the proportion of school-leavers according to the type of formal qualification obtained (see Table III) clearly confirm the trend towards the highest possible school-leaving qualification. Between 1960 and 1994 the proportion of school-leavers without any school-leaving certificate and with a Hauptschule-certificate decreased by half. The proportion of school-leavers with an intermediate school-leaving certificate or an equivalent qualification (Realschule) or an entrance qualification for institutions of higher education has tripled; those attaining a qualification for university entrance even quadrupled in the same period.

Type of qualification	1960	1970	1980	1990	1994*
	%	%	%	%	%
Without short-course secondary school-leaving certificate (Hauptschule)	17.2	17.3	10.2	8.6	8.7
With short-course secondary school-leaving certificate (Hauptschule)	53.4	43.0	36.6	32.0	26.0
With intermediate school-leaving certificate or equivalent (Realschule)	15.1	24.9	39.2	44.0	44.7
Both with restricted and general university entrance quaification (Fachabitur und Abitur)	6.1	11.3	21.7	33.5	34.9
With general university entrance qualification only (allgemeine Hochschulreife/Abitur)	6.1	10.7	16.5	24.4	25.9

Table III. School-leavers from general and vocational schools according to the type of qualification obtained, expressed as a percentage of the population of the same age group. 1960-1990 the former Federal Republic of Germany only. Source: Der Bundesminister für Bildung, Wissenschaft, Forschung und Technologie (Ed.) Grund- und Strukturdaten, 1995-1996, pp. 84-85. *1994: Germany, now including East Germany.

The increase in the proportion of school-leavers with the Abitur is a result of both the increased enrolment rates at Gymnasien and the decrease in selectivity practised by this school type. Analyses of the data for successive age-groups show that the chance of remaining in and of successfully completing a Gymnasium has increased (Hansen & Rolff, 1990). Regarding the transfers between types of schools in general, empirical studies show that more than 90 per cent of the pupils of a given age-group remain at the chosen school type (Blossfeld, 1988). This general trend in the choice of school type and the formal school-leaving qualification outlined above masks important differences between genders, social classes, ethnic groups and regions.

Gender-specific Differences

The expansion of the general school system at the secondary school level since the 1960s can to a significant extent be attributed to the fact that the enrolment rates of girls increased considerably at Realschulen and Gymnasien (Köhler, 1990, p. 47ff, p. 117). As shown in Table IV, in 1994 the proportion of female school-leavers with the Abitur exceeded the respective proportion of male school-leavers [1].

Type of qualification	1967	1970	1980	1990	1994*
	%	%	%	%	%
Without short-course secondary school-leaving certificate (Hauptschule)	44.3	44.5	38.1	38.9	35.6
With short-course secondary school-leaving certificate (Hauptschule)	50.3	49.3	45.8	44.2	43.1
With intermediate school-leaving certificate or equivalent (Realschule)	50.5	51.6	55.4	52.3	51.4
Both with restricted and general university entrance quaification (Fachabitur und Abitur)	36.5	39.4	45.4	46.3	49.9
Of which with general university entrance qualification only (allgemeine Hochschulreife/Abitur)	36.5	39.4	48.5	49.5	52.5

Table IV. Proportion of female school-leavers from general and vocational schools according to the type of qualification obtained, expressed as a percentage of the respective total school-leaving population. 1967-1990 the former Federal Republic of Germany only. Source: Der Bundesminister für Bildung, Wissenschaft, Forschung und Technologie (Ed.) Grund- und Strukturdaten, 1995-1996, pp. 86-87. *1994: Germany, now including East Germany.

Regional Differences

The regional disparities existing in school provision (differences in access to a school supply comprising the full range of school-leaving certificates) have important implications for educational participation in addition to the regional socio-economic and socio-demographic contexts. Rural areas with an incomplete supply of secondary schools have significantly lower participation rates of pupils in the more highly rated types of secondary schools (i.e. lower levels of formal qualification are obtained) than urban areas. The relative proportion of school attendance at Gymnasien in city states with a diverse school structure and 'quasi-markets' also exceeds those in the Länder (Flächenstaaten). At the local level studies have repeatedly shown that both educational aspirations and participation are positively correlated with community size and schools' proximity to home (Steinert et al, 1992; Ditton, 1995). At the Länder level the proportion of pupils enrolled at different secondary school types varies with the specific macro-school structure which depends on tradition and long-term educational policy.

Ethnic Differences

Significant differences in educational participation and the school qualification obtained exist between German and foreign pupils and between the different nationalities of migrant workers. In comparison to the German school population foreign pupils are under-represented at Gymnasien and over-represented at special schools for educationally handicapped children (Sonderschulen für Lernbehinderte) and at Hauptschulen. Among the individual nationalities more pupils from Greece, Portugal, Spain and the former Yugoslavia than the average total number of foreign pupils obtain a middle school-leaving certificate, whereas pupils from Italy and Turkey more frequently leave school without any certificate or with the Hauptschule-certificate only (Köhler, 1990, p. 29ff; Hornberg, 1992, p. 243; Alba et al, 1994, p. 216ff).

Social Differences

The parents' educational aspirations and preferences for a certain type of secondary school vary significantly with their occupational status and their educational qualification. In 1993 nearly 80 per cent of the parents employed as civil servants wanted their children to obtain the highest school-leaving certificate, the Abitur, as compared to 26 per cent of working-class parents (Rolff et al, 1994b, p. 19ff). The picture gained from data on parents' educational aspiration corresponds (at a lower level) to the figures on the enrolment rates of 13-14 year-olds according to the type of secondary school (Table V).

Social position of the head of the family	Relative school attendance of the population of 13 and 14 year-olds					
	Short-course secondary school (Hauptschule)		Intermediate school (Realschule)		Grammar school (Gymnasium)	
	1976 %	1989 %	1976 %	1989 %	1976 %	1989 %
Self-employed	**45.7**	**31.6**	**24.7**	**27.7**	**25.1**	**37.1**
Others, non-academic self-employed	61.7	46.5	23.1	35.8	10.9	15.6
Self-employed farmers	35.6	33.4	27.3	29.1	32.0	33.0
Self-employed academics	(4.1)	(2.0)	(11.1)	(10.0)	84.8	84.8
Civil servants	**25.7**	**14.0**	**22.5**	**24.2**	**47.4**	**57.4**
Civil servants without a middle qualification*	38.5	27.5	30.2	37.3	26.1	32.1
Civil servants with a middle qualification*	21.8	(13.2)	23.5	32.3	50.3	49.4
Civil servants with Abitur	(7.4)	(6.7)	(9.0)	11.9	80.6	76.8
Employees	**32.1**	**22.1**	**24.7**	**29.8**	**37.8**	**42.8**
Employees without a middle qualification*	40.5	32.5	26.9	33.1	26.8	28.9
Employees with a middle qualification*	22.3	16.4	23.6	30.9	49.6	47.7
Employees with Abitur	11.7	(7.6)	16.0	19.7	67.3	67.1
Workers	**64.2**	**58.3**	**19.5**	**26.0**	**9.3**	**10.8**
German workers without apprenticeship	69.5	65.4	18.1	21.3	5.9	7.8
German workers with apprenticeship	59.7	52.2	21.9	30.4	11.7	12.8
Foriegn workers without apprenticeship	77.0	71.2	(6.6)	16.3	(2.7)	7.7
Foriegn workers with apprenticeship	78.8	58.3	(6.1)	25.9	(6.5)	(10.0)
Others	**65.1**	**56.2**	**13.8**	**22.2**	**13.7**	**15.7**
Total	**50.1**	**39.6**	**21.4**	**26.8**	**22.5**	**28.7**

Table V. Relative school attendance of the population of 13 and 14 year-olds according to social backgrounds, 1976 and 1989. *Intermediate school-leaving certificate (Realschule) or equivalent qualification. ( ) Cells contain fewer than 50 cases. Source: Statistisches Bundesamt. Special analysis based on the Microsensus for the Max Planck Institute for Human Development and Education. Source: Köhler, 1992, p. 55.

The figures in Table V show that in accordance with international experiences (e.g. Blossfeld & Shavit, 1993) no substantial reduction of social inequalities was achieved in the period 1976-1989. The relationship between social background and educational participation is even stronger when the educational qualification of parents is used as social status indicator. The educational disadvantages of pupils from the lower social strata that still exist have multiple causes which cannot be discussed in detail (see for example Ditton, 1995). Finally, the difference in economic, cultural and social capital (Bourdieu) is of decisive importance in planning one's life in general and school careers in particular. Differences in these types of capital manifest themselves in different cognitive, motivational and linguistic competencies imparted through the family socialisation process. The demands of the Gymnasium with regard to these competencies are geared towards the middle class (Hurrelmann, 1985). The findings of an empirical study by Fend (1982) on the educational participation of children with different abilities belonging to different social groups illustrate the influence that this obstacle has on the educational choice of low status parents. According to this study, the chances that a highly intelligent working-class child attends a Gymnasium is nearly one third lower than the chances of the least intelligent children from middle and upper social class backgrounds. This finding is also supported by research that indicates more stable educational aspirations and a greater ability to enforce their aspirations among parents from the higher social strata: they are less dependent on the primary school teacher's recommendations, are more prone to have their child continue its school career at a Gymnasium in the case of inadequate achievement and to switch to the less demanding Realschule only if it has become impossible for their child to remain at the Gymnasium any longer. Apart from that parents' aspirations are more easily attained because of the fact that pupils from privileged social backgrounds benefit from biases in the marking practices of teachers, which are obviously influenced by a stereotyped perception of the abilities and achievements of pupils from different social backgrounds (Ditton, 1995).

Quasi-markets and Parental School Choice

In educational quasi-markets the following trends can be identified with regard to the individual school types:

1. The particular competitive situation facing the short-course secondary school (Hauptschule) leads to an enrolment ratio that is significantly below the state-wide average for this school type, particularly when it coincides with a socio-economic environment that is to its disadvantage (high professional qualifications and – related to this – educational aspirations of the population, high qualification demands of the labour market). The Hauptschule is even less accepted if comprehensive schools are available as equivalent fourth

school type. Many short-course secondary schools (Hauptschulen) would have had to be closed down if an unrestricted market mechanism had been in effect. Counteracting this mechanism for political reasons many short-course secondary schools are being maintained artificially – with school sizes that are no longer tolerable pedagogically and economically. In some conurbations with a high proportion of migrant families the position of short-course secondary schools could be backed up because a disproportional number of these families choose this school type. However, these schools tend to become 'schools for the leftovers' in which the main problem groups are concentrated: socially disadvantaged German pupils, pupils with learning disabilities and foreign children from different origins and with a low command of the German language who sometimes represent more than three-quarters of the pupil population at these schools. In such an environment of negatively selected pupils improvements in schooling can hardly succeed. Expensive measures of 'positive discrimination' (e.g. improving the standard of equipment, extending the curricular and extra-curricular offers) have not been able to stop the dwindling attractiveness of the short-course secondary school. Many thus speak of this school as an 'expiring model'.

2. The unchallenged 'market leader' in the esteem of parents is the Gymnasium which offers the most attractive schooling as it qualifies for entrance to universities. Although this school-leaving qualification can also be obtained via other school types – comprehensive schools and intermediate schools – if a student's achievement level meets the admission requirements for the upper level of the Gymnasium, the overwhelming majority of parents who want their children to obtain the Abitur choose the direct way ('royal road') by sending their children to a Gymnasium. The essential reasons for parents are: avoiding having to transfer their child to another school after the 10th grade, the achievement orientation and the prestigious image of the Gymnasium, and placing their children in a setting that offers the preferred social and cultural milieu. Together with the socio-economic context the relatively favourable supply situation explains the disproportionally high enrolment rates at the Gymnasium in the urban educational market. One of the most striking phenomena is that the transfer ratio to the Gymnasium is particularly high in those areas in whose vicinity comprehensive schools have been established. The competition between these two types of schools, which flared up in the period of demographic decline, has created an 'attraction effect' because many Gymnasien, anxious not to operate at undercapacity and to avoid possible closure, showed a market-like behaviour by developing advertising activities. In view of the high educational aspirations of parents one can assume that the run on the Gymnasium will continue. All school types in the educational market will be affected by this development, not least of all the Gymnasium itself. Having already lost the character of an elite institution in the course of the educational expansion in the 1960s and

1970s, the Gymnasium is on the way to becoming the new 'general school', that is, the school that the major proportion of pupils at secondary level will be attending. The changing clientele accompanying this process will have consequences for both the Gymnasium's achievement profile and its mission, which can no longer be exclusively geared to the preparation for academic studies.[2] One reaction to this development was a greater differentiation between schools. Partly this was guided by the intention of regaining exclusivity by developing special curricular profiles (e.g. bilingual instruction, different sequences in foreign language teaching), targeted at the traditional clientele of the Gymnasium, the education-conscious middle class. Those sections of this group that value the 'fine distinctions' (Bourdieu) have partly reacted to the loss of exclusivity of the average Gymnasium by sending their children to traditional classical or private Gymnasien.

(3) The comprehensive school is winner and loser at the same time: winner in comparison to the short-course secondary school (Hauptschule) and loser in comparison to the Gymnasium and frequently also to the organizationally independent intermediate school (Realschule) which competes for the same clientele. The comprehensive school has not managed to become generally accepted as an alternative to the tripartite school system in the educational market. Its acceptance by parents with children capable of attending a Gymnasium is very low: only a few of the pupils who are recommended for the Gymnasium by the primary school transfer to a comprehensive if a Gymnasium is available.[3] The negative image of the comprehensive school is strongly shaped by the controversial public debate on this school type.[4] It is, however, an attractive alternative for those parents whose children show a 'broken' achievement profile in the three most important subjects (German, Mathematics and Elementary Science) in primary school and who consider the risk of failing in the Gymnasium to be very high. The 'creaming effect' apparent at comprehensive schools as a result of the competition from the Gymnasium has the consequence that the goal of achieving social integration through pupil populations of mixed ability, which was the main impetus for the introduction of comprehensives, has not been attained. This goal will only be achieved if comprehensive schools – screened off from the competition of the Gymnasium – are the only schools provided or if they have a unique position in the educational market with a profile as model or alternative school for educationally committed parents. It has also been shown that comprehensive schools affected by the 'creaming effect' can recruit pupils (even high achievers) through 'niche marketing', that is, if they fill a market gap by developing a profile that is targeted at the specific needs of particular groups of the student population in their catchment area, e.g. by providing special care-taking services, special supportive measures for pupils with poor knowledge of German, homework assistance etc. (see Rauin & Weishaupt 1991). There is also evidence that the competitive disadvantage is partially compensated for by lowering performance standards. At any rate, the

discrepancy between the low proportion of high achievers at many comprehensive schools and the frequently high ratio of pupils given the right to attend the Gymnasium upper level grades is particularly striking.[5]

4. Up to now the intermediate school (Realschule) has been able to maintain its position. Like the Gymnasium the profile of the Realschule has, however, changed fundamentally. It appears that under educational market conditions the intermediate school has the most heterogeneous student body with regard to abilities (compare Klemm & Rolff, 1988, pp. 68-69). Viewed from a purely quantitative perspective the intermediate school could benefit from two future developments: first from the growing educational aspirations of (second generation) migrant families, and second from overcrowding at Gymnasien which could increase the number of pupils rejected. This would, however, aggravate the pedagogical problems at intermediate schools.

Actual Developments and Future Perspectives

In accordance with international developments pluralization and autonomy, decentralization and parent empowerment, greater responsiveness to clients and supply-side differentiation have become the new guiding principles of educational policy in Germany. This reorientation, labelled by some observers as a paradigm shift, was on the one hand a response to the political system's loss of legitimation and the conflict-ridden state of education policy in Germany (compare Weiss, 1993). An important impetus came, on the other hand, from the insights gained from implementation and school effectiveness research on success of innovations and the profile of 'effective' schools, which brought individual schools as the 'pedagogic units of action' (Fend, 1986) into the centre of attention. The centralist-administrative strategy of large-scale reforms aimed at changing the macro-structure of the school system was replaced by a decentralised micro-level reform strategy.[6]

As a consequence of the paradigm shift 'from school structure to school culture' (Leschinsky, 1992) any attempts to reach a general consensus on the (structural) development of the German school system were abolished in favour of the particularistic policies of the individual Länder.[7] School reform was continued as 'piecemeal engineering' on a small scale at grassroots level. Conducive to this was the extension of decision-making competence and responsibility to the individual school, which initially was considered to work as a strategy of 'compensatory legitimation' (Weiler, 1989) by relieving the overtaxed political system of conflict regulation and at the same time meeting the growing demand for participation and self-determination in society (for details, see Weiss, 1993).

Several Länder have decided on strengthening school autonomy by granting schools a greater scope of action in pedagogical, curricular, organisational and resource allocation matters and have amended their school laws recently. Schools nonetheless remain   in accordance with the constitution under the control of the state, that is the individual Land, which is responsible for essential decisions concerning the school system as a whole (e.g. curricula, school-leaving certificates, the macro-structure of the educational system, teacher training and appointments, for details, see Avenarius, 1994 and 1995). The authority to decide on personnel and financial resources also still rests with the state (or the community). The concepts of autonomy, however, usually allow for the allocation of a global budget, restricted to operating expenditure, by the providing body (community, district) to enable the schools to utilize the financial resources according to their specific preferences and needs.

In the course of extending school autonomy the position of parents has also been strengthened regarding school choice and their participation in school-based decision-making. The authority to decide what type of secondary school their child will attend after primary school legally rests with the parents. In practice, however, the recommendation of the primary school teacher plays a major role in the parents' decision. As mentioned above, until recently specific achievement requirements (an examination or a trial period of instruction) were necessary if – contrary to the primary school recommendation – parents wanted their child to attend a school leading to university entrance qualification (Abitur). A number of Länder have revoked this requirement in the meantime, thus giving parents the full authority over their child's school career. Another important step towards the empowerment of parents is their involvement in the management of schools which some Länder have recently decided on by establishing the 'school conference', in which teachers, parents and (at the secondary school level) pupils are represented, as another directing body besides the principal and the teaching staff conference. The competencies assigned to the school conference comprise curricular, pedagogical and organisational issues of strategic relevance for the development of a school-specific profile.

Giving parents a free choice of the type of secondary school will force schools to become more responsive to the needs and preferences of parents. The strengthening of school autonomy and the institutionalisation of a new directing body in which parents can bring their interests to bear were important measures to increase the 'demand side orientation' of schools. Notwithstanding the fact that in Germany the driving force behind the outlined reform process was not the market ideology, this process undoubtedly will reinforce the trend towards a market-governed school system with growing competition between schools and increasing diversity of supply beyond the formal differentiation given by the tripartite (or four-part) school structure. One consequence of this development might be a further fragmentation and hierarchisation of the school system. Whereas this effect would be the result of 'market forces', the already existing hierarchy is a result of policy decisions.

But these decisions are increasingly proving problematic. There is sufficient evidence that the traditional tripartite school system with separately operating school units cannot adjust effectively to shifts in educational demand and that the coexistence of different competing secondary schools at lower-secondary level tends to increase total system costs. In view of the precarious fiscal situation and efforts to cope with the 'cost disease' in education, the obvious wastage of personnel resources caused by an uneconomic school structure has become an issue of growing concern.[8] The pressure to enforce the 'economic principle' in education and to 'consolidate' the diverse school provision exerted especially by the Länder audit offices (cf. Weiss, 1992) is in conflict with an educational policy that is urging the principle of pluralism in order to respond to differentiated educational demands. The significant shift in educational aspirations and the need to relieve the state budget have put the question of school structure which was hotly debated in the 1970s in connection with the proposed replacement of the tripartite secondary school system with a comprehensive one back onto the political agenda. It can be expected that the fiscal austerity situation all Länder are facing will in the future make it easier to discuss the school structure issue in a less ideologically biased way than in the 1970s. In the East German Länder the 'demographic implosion' demands new solutions.[9] School closures and the establishment of multigrade primary schools in sparsely populated rural areas will be unavoidable. At the lower-secondary level, where several school types compete for a steadily decreasing number of pupils, the existence of the schools ranked below the Gymnasium (or the corresponding tracks in comprehensive schools) will be jeopardised. The majority of the West German Länder governments so far are hesitant to tackle overdue structural adaptations necessary to accommodate to the changed demand constellation. In a few Länder, however, promising measures have been initiated, for example, the introduction of 'Regional Schools' in Rhineland-Palatinate, which combine Hauptschulen and Realschulen.[10] As a reaction to the significant loss of attractiveness of the Hauptschule the parliament of the state of Saarland recently amended its constitution with the votes of the conservative opposition by removing the Hauptschule as a regular type of school. These examples mark the first step towards the development of attractive alternatives to the Gymnasium within a 'bipartite school structure'. It could eventually lead to a system of two formally equivalent types of school as proposed by some educationists. According to Hurrelmann (1988), alongside the Gymnasium, with its preparatory-study orientation toward academic subjects, a new kind of comprehensive school should be established as an alternative, one that combines vocational and general educational curricular contents (practical and theoretical learning) and also provides the opportunity to attain (in addition to all other school-leaving certificates) the Abitur. In so doing equality in the competitive ability of schools, which to a large extent depends on the kind of school-leaving qualification they award, would at least be achieved formally. Whether these new schools, which lack the 'goodwill' of the traditional Gymnasien, would be able to assert their position in direct competition with these, is an open question. The two types of school are geared to different abilities and would attract parents from different socio-cultural backgrounds. Parents' school choice behaviour indicates a strong preference for selective schools within a hierarchically structured system. If policy-makers should ever change this situation fundamentally (which seems highly improbable), the market acting in combination with an empowered demand side would enforce an educational supply according to consumers' preferences. And these preferences are heavily influenced by the growing expectation that schools change from governmental institutions to service agencies. If the state schools cannot adapt adequately to this new role, the (highly subsidised) private school sector (compare Weiss & Mattern, 1989) could gain growing importance, all the more so as budget cuts in the wake of the likely aggravation of the fiscal crisis would be perceived as a deterioration in the quality of the state school system.

Notes

[1] In higher education women are still under-represented, although differences decreased in the last few years. In vocational training (in the Dual System) girls are also still at a disadvantage.

[2] Studies conducted during the mid-1980s in North Rhine-Westphalia and Baden-Württemberg showed that only between two-thirds and three-quarters of the pupils enrolled in the fifth grade of a Gymnasium obtained their Abitur in grade 13 and that of these only about 70 per cent took up university studies (Klemm & Rolff, 1988, p. 82).

[3] Studies in Dortmund have shown that nearly 90 per cent of the parents of fourth graders with the best marks (an average of 2 or better) send their children to the Gymnasium. Only 5 per cent choose the comprehensive school (Hansen & Rolff, 1990).

[4] In representative opinion polls the comprehensive school is regularly given the lowest ratings: about one-third of the respondents give it the worst grade of 4-6 (Gymnasium: 9 per cent). Grades 1 or 2 are awarded by only about 40 per cent (Gymnasium: just under 70 per cent – compare Rolff et al, 1990, p. 27).

[5] This, by the way, refutes the belief of market ideologists that competition in educational markets will bring about quality improvements for all schools.

[6] This strategy was also suggested by the results of empirical studies comparing the climate and effectiveness of secondary schools of the tripartite system (Hauptschule, Realschule, Gymnasium) and comprehensive schools. They revealed that differences between the schools within each group (tripartite/comprehensive) were greater than between the two groups of schools compared (Fend, 1982).

[7] The failure to update the Comprehensive Education Development Plan is the most striking example (for details, see Weiss & Weishaupt, 1990).

[8] Of decisive importance in this direction was a widely publicised expert report compiled by a private management consultancy firm on the state of the school system in North-Rhine-Westphalia ('Kienbaum Expert Report').

[9] In the East German Länder the number of first-graders will decrease from about 200,000 to 85,000 by the year 2000.

[10] For economic reasons some Länder started to reduce the scope of internal choice for pupils at upper-secondary level of Gymnasien by cutting back the range of courses offered (courses with low enrolment numbers). Partly schools returned to class instruction, introduced multi-grade courses or established courses (e.g. in certain foreign languages) in cooperation with other schools.

References

Alba, R.D., Handl, J., & Müller, W. (1994) Ethnische Ungleichheit im deutschen Bildungssystem, *Kölner Zeitschrift für Soziologie und Sozialpsychologie*, 46, pp. 209-237.

Avenarius, H. (1994) Schulische Selbstverwaltung Grenzen und Möglichkeiten, *Recht der Jugend und des Bildungswesens*, 42, pp. 256-269.

Avenarius, H. (1995) Educational decision-making in open societies: the case of West and East Germany, in P.M. Roeder, I. Richter, H.-P. Füssel (Eds) *Pluralism and education: current world trends in policy, law and administration* Berlin: Max Planck Institute for Human Development and Education.

Bargel, T. & Kuthe, M. (1992) Regionale Disparitäten und Ungleichheiten im Schulwesen, in P. Zedler (Ed.) *Strukturprobleme. Disparitäten. Grundbildung in der Sekundarstufe I.* Weinheim: Deutscher Studien Verlag.

Bargel, T. & Kuthe, M. (1993) Schulstruktur und regionale Schulversorgung: das Lehrstück Baden-Württemberg, *Pädagogische Führung*, 4, pp. 50-55.

Blossfeld, H.-P. (1988) Sensible Phasen im Bildungsverlauf. Eine Längsschnittanalyse über die Prägung von Bildungskarrieren durch den gesellschaftlichen Wandel, *Zeitschrift für Pädagogik*, 34, pp. 45-64.

Blossfeld, H.-P., & Shavit, Y. (1993) Dauerhafte Ungleichheiten. Zur Veränderung des Einflusses der sozialen Herkunft auf die Bildungschancen in dreizehn industrialisierten Ländern, *Zeitschrift für Pädagogik*, 39, pp. 25-52.

Bundesminister für Bildung und Wissenschaft (Ed.) (1992/93) Grund- und Strukturdaten 1992/93, Bonn.

Bundesminister für Bildung, Wissenschaft, Forschung und Technologie (Ed.) (1995/96) Grund- und Strukturdaten 1995/96, Bonn.

Ditton, H. (1995) Ungleichheitsforschung, in H.-G. Rolff (Ed.) *Zukunftsfelder der Schulforschung.* Weinheim: Deutscher Studien Verlag.

Fend, H. (1982) *Gesamtschule im Vergleich.* Weinheim: Beltz.

Fend, H. (1986) 'Gute Schulen, schlechte Schulen'. Die einzelne Schule als pädagogische Handlungseinheit, *Die Deutsche Schule*, 82, pp. 275-293.

Führ, Ch. (1992) *On the Education System in the Five new Länder of the Federal Republic of Germany.* Bonn: Inter Nationes.

Hansen, R. & Rolff, H.-G. (1990) 'Abgeschwächte Auslese und verschärfter Wettbewerb – Neuere Entwicklungen in den Sekundarschulen' in H.-G. Rolff et al (Eds) *Jahrbuch der Schulentwicklung*, vol. 6. Weinheim: Juventa.

Hornberg, S. (1992) Multikulturelle Schülerschaft in der neuen Bundesrepublik, in H.-G. Rolff et al (Eds) *Jahrbuch der Schulentwicklung*, vol. 7. Weinheim: Juventa.

Hurrelmann, K. (1985) Soziale Ungleichheit und Selektion im Erziehungssystem. Ergebnisse und Implikationen der sozialstrukturellen Sozialisationsforschung, in H. Strasser & J.H. Goldthorpe (Eds) *Die Analyse der sozialen Ungleichheit.* Opladen: Westdeutscher Verlag.

Hurrelmann, K. (1988) 'Thesen zur strukturellen Entwicklung des Bildungssystems in den nächsten fünf bis zehn Jahren, *Die Deutsche Schule*, 80, pp. 451-461.

Klemm, K. & Rolff, H.-G. (1988) Der heimliche Umbau der Sekundarschule, in H.-G. Rolff et al. (Eds) *Jahrbuch der Schulentwicklung,* vol. 5. Weinheim: Juventa.

Köhler, H. (1990) *Neue Entwicklungen des relativen Schul- und Hochschulbesuchs. Eine Analyse der Daten für 1975-1987,* Materialien aus der Bildungsforschung No. 37. Berlin: Max Planck Institute for Human Development and Education.

Köhler, H. (1992) *Bildungsbeteiligung und Sozialstruktur in der Bundesrepublik. Zu Stabilität und Wandel der Ungleichheit von Bildungschancen.* Studien und Berichte, 53. Berlin: Max Planck Institute for Human Development and Education.

Leschinsky, A. (1992) Dezentralisierung im Schulsystem der Bundesrepublik Deutschland, in P. Zedler (Ed.) *Strukturprobleme, Disparitäten, Grundbildung in der Sekundarstufe I.* Weinheim: Deutscher Studien Verlag.

Leschinsky, A. (1994) Freie Schulwahl und staatliche Steuerung. Neue Regelungen des Übergangs an weiterführenden Schulen, *Zeitschrift für Pädagogik,* 40, pp. 963-981.

Rauin, U. & Weishaupt, H. (1991) Schulangebot und Elternwille. Probleme der Gesamtschulentwicklung in Hessen am Beispiel des Landkreises Groß-Gerau, unpublished paper. Frankfurt: German Institute for International Educational Research.

Rolff, H.-G. et al (Eds) (1990) *Jahrbuch der Schulentwicklung,* vol. 6. Weinheim: Juventa.

Rolff, H.-G. (1994a)'Steuerung und Beratung der Schulentwicklung in Europa – Theorien und Fallstudien, in 32. Beiheft der Zeitschrift für Pädagogik, *Bildung und Erziehung in Europa.* Weinheim: Beltz.

Rolff, H.-G. et al (Eds) (1994b) *Jahrbuch der Schulentwicklung,* vol. 8. Weinheim: Juventa.

Sekretariat der Ständigen Konkerenz der Kultusminister der Länder in der Bundesrepublik Deutschland (KMK) (Ed.) (1994) *Schüler, Klassen, Lehrer und Absolventen der Schulen 1984-1993, Statistische Veröffentlichungen der Kultusministerkonferenz,* Dokumentation No. 129. Bonn.

Steinert, B., Raun, U. & Weishaupt, H. (1992) *Rahmenbedingungen für mehr Schulqualität in Hessen: Modellrechnungen zur Schulentwicklung in den 90er Jahren.* Frankfurt a.M.: German Institute for International Educational Research.

Weiler, H.N. (1989) Why reforms fail: the politics of education in France and the Federal Republic of Germany, *Journal of Curriculum Studies,* 21, pp. 291-305.

Weiss, M. (1992) Zur inneren Ökonomie des Schulwesens, *Recht der Jugend und des Bildungswesens,* 40, pp. 206-217.

Weiss, M. (1993) New guiding principles in educational policy: the case of Germany, *Journal of Educational Policy,* 8, pp. 307-320.

Weiss, M. & Mattern, C. (1989) The situation and development of the private school system in Germany, in G. Walford (Ed.) *Private Schools in Ten Countries.* London: Routledge.

Weiss, M. & Weidhaupt, H. (1990) Experiences with comprehensive educational planning: lessons from the Federal Republic of Germany, *European Journal of Education,* 25, pp. 83-87.

Oxford Studies in Comparative Education, Vol. 6(1), 1996

School Choice in the United States: possessive individualism, educational deregulation, and the public good

PETER W. COOKSON, Jr

Thunder on the Right

Not far from the Capitol building in Washington DC is one of the largest and poorest African-American ghettos in North America. Washington is a 'de facto' apartheid city; the affluent, influential, and socially mobile white city contrasts sharply with the poor, powerless, and economically stagnant African-American city. The American Capital is located in the District of Columbia, which is neither a state nor a protectorate, but an extension of the federal government; its budget is established by the United States House of Representatives. In early November 1995, a spending Bill for the District was debated on the floor of the House. Included in the Bill was a federally financed school voucher program – a voucher is any system of certificate or cash payments by the government that enables students to attend schools of their choice, public or private. Generally, vouchers have a fixed value and are redeemed at the time of enrolment. The DC Bill would permit a small number of city public school students to attend private or suburban public schools. The Speaker of the House, Newt Gingrich (Republican, Georgia), made a fiery speech on the floor of the House, "We should quit requiring the children of DC to go to violent schools, drug-ridden schools, and schools that are dens of illiteracy and dens of ignorance. We should give them a chance to have a scholarship and go to a decent place" (Clines, 1995, A22). Opposition to the voucher proposal was sharp; Representative Julian C. Dickson (Democrat, California) said, "We should improve the public schools in the District of Columbia, that is where the problem is. There are not enough resources in the country to give vouchers or scholarships to all the needy children" (Clines, 1995).

The voucher allotment provided by the Bill is up to $3000 per child – roughly $5000 short of the average tuition of the private schools in the District. Speaker Gingrich defended the Bill by asking, "Whether you are for the poorest children in DC in the poorest neighbourhoods in the worst schools having the same opportunity as the Gore family, the same opportunity as the President's family" (Clines, 1995). The House adopted the voucher program by a vote of 241 to 177, as an amendment to the District's annual budget appropriation. The action of the House signifies how much school choice and the deregulation of public education has defined the American school reform agenda. Virtually every state in the Union has either enacted school choice legislation or is contemplating such legislation (Cookson, 1994a; Henig, 1994).

The most common school choice plans are intra-sectional, providing choice between public schools. Within this context there has been a 'revolution' in terms of how public schools are governed; the charter school movement, in particular, has considerable strength in such diverse states as Florida, Minnesota, Massachusetts, California, Wisconsin, and Louisiana. There is a growing tendency, however, for reformers and legislators to suggest intersectional choice plans whereby public funds finance private schools. A variety of groups support intersectional choice, including civil libertarians, religious fundamentalists, market-oriented reformers, and fiscal conservatives. Intersectional choice legislation has been placed on the ballot in California, Ohio, Minnesota, Oregon, Colorado, and Pennsylvania. In 1992 former President George Bush introduced a national voucher program entitled the 'G.I. Bill Opportunity Scholarships for Children.' Since 1991 there has been a pilot voucher plan in the state of Wisconsin called the Milwaukee Parental Choice Program. Church and state are constitutionally separated in the United States; therefore, intersectional choice plans raise many legal issues because the majority of American private schools are sectarian (Kemerer, 1995).

The only other country to have experimented so widely with privatization and school choice is the United Kingdom (Walford, 1992). Yet, I think it safe to say that if political trends remain as they are the American experience with educational deregulation will make the British market experiment seem modest and tentative (Hakim et a.l, 1994; Lieberman, 1989; duPont, 1994; Chubb & Moe, 1990). I say this because Americans have historically supported separatist local forms of governance and relied on the market to provide public goods (Cookson, 1992). American political life is suspicious of authority and periodically xenophobic, creating a public culture distrustful of public institutions (Hofstadter, 1966).

This essay is an examination of market-oriented school choice in the United States. The data are drawn from a variety of sources touching on the extent of school choice, the effects of school choice, and the underlying assumptions of those who propose to deregulate public education. The organization of the paper is straightforward. Section One is a brief overview of the landscape of American education, its relationship to the market, and a summary of popular opinion about school choice. Section Two provides an historical and theoretical framework for understanding why the deregulation and commercialization of public education has an appeal to so many policy-makers, politicians, and other agents of symbolic control. Section Three is an examination of the major choice plans in the United States that rely on market principles of organization. Section Four is a review of the most recent empirical evidence about the relationship of market reforms to student achievement. Section Five is a summary statement about the dangers of mistaking the public good with the economic welfare of the already privileged and how this mistake, if not corrected, could destroy democratically controlled education.

The Landscape of American Education

One of the ironies of the current choice debate in the United States is that public education is by no means as centralized or as ineffective as its critics claim (Rothstein, 1993; Berliner & Biddle, 1995; Carnegie Foundation, 1992). In terms of centralization, the United States does not have a federal ministry of education; the Department of Education has virtually no authority over schools except in terms of enforcing civil rights laws and regulations. In 1992, the federal government contributed 8.3 per cent of the expenditure for all levels of education. As a percentage of expenditures for elementary and secondary education, the federal share is 5.6 (Cookson, 1995; Irwin, 1992). Each state is constitutionally responsible for its schools, and it is through tax levied dollars obtained at the state and local levels that public education is primarily financed.

Because of this decentralization, American education is far from 'monopolistic' (Witte, 1990:13). There are over 15,000 public school districts in the United States, comprising approximately 60,000 elementary schools, and over 23,000 secondary schools (Witte, 1990, p. 15). Public school districts vary in size and there is a great deal of variation in the grade organization of schools. In terms of curriculum and pedagogy, there are no monopolistic practices in the United States. As public school critics Arthur Powell, Eleanor Farrar, and David Cohen point out in *The Shopping Mall High School* (1985), American education is a cacophony of curricula and teaching styles. Compared to France, Germany, or Japan, the American public school system is radically decentralized, teacher-driven, and wondrously chaotic.

For a decade and a half public education in the United States has been under attack, particularly by conservatives, religious fundamentalists, libertarians, and corporate leaders. They claim that the United States is 'at risk' because its schools are so poor. As evidence of poor performance, they cite high drop-out rates, low scores on standardized tests, school violence, and technical illiteracy among graduates. They claim that these problems do not stem from underfunding, but from self-interested public school bureaucracies that are expensive, and block innovation. Recently, these claims have been challenged (Berliner & Biddle, 1995; Bracey, 1994; Rothstein, 1993). The efficacy and fairness of the American school system will remain a matter of debate for some time, but whatever the empirical truth of the competing claims, the deregulators have been astute in the realm of public relations, calling into question virtually all of the policies supporting public education and the welfare state (Cookson, 1996). This is ironic because in the United States the public sector is pitifully small compared to the private sector. While public institutions are portrayed as 'greedy,' private institutions seem immune from criticism. This is peculiar because the division between the rich and the poor in the United States is the most extreme of any industrialized country and the real value of wages in terms of purchasing power has declined significantly in the last 20 years (Phillips, 1990; Persell & Cookson, 1992). For many Americans the social frontier is closing.

Despite the claims by the political right that public schools are a monopoly, education in the United States is really a quasi-public institution; for over 150 years publicly funded education and private education have coexisted, and 12 per cent of American students attend private schools. Moreover, many private schools receive public dollars to support specific educational activities including special education programs, transportation, and surplus food programs. In the emerging quasi-market governance structure education is no longer a public good in the strict sense. On the contrary, it is a private good. In a quasi-market, education ceases to be a collective responsibility and becomes a matter of individual rights. In the traditional quasi-public system educational opportunity is a positive 'liberty' that the state makes available to citizens. In a quasi-market system, liberty is defined negatively as freedom from state control, although most educational entrepreneurs appear willing to accept public funds for their enterprises. With the exception of national defense, most public service organizations are considered by the market coalition as inefficient, corrupt, and corrupting of initiative and ambition. Perhaps because this argument lends ideological support to powerful business interests, it has gained wider acceptance than one might expect.

Americans in general, however, are quite supportive of public education. According to a 1995 Phi Delta Kappa/Gallup Poll, most Americans continue to rate the schools in their own communities quite highly; significantly, the closer people get to the schools, the higher the ratings. Almost two-thirds of public school parents assign a grade of A or B to the school their oldest child attends (Elam & Rose, 1995, p. 41). Support for intrasectional choice is strong; however, intersectional choice is generally opposed. People believe that private schools which accept public funds should be subject to regulation by public authorities. In other words, while conservative policy-makers, libertarians, and market advocates are singing the praises of competition, most Americans remain faithful to the neighbourhood school and for all that implies about local control, democracy, and equality of educational opportunity. Yet, the siren of the market calls to some Americans, bewitching them by holding out the promise of prosperity based on private property.

The American Enlightenment: private property as the foundation of the public good

The American Revolution was in some ways unique. Animated by a passion for liberty and a deep suspicion of human nature, the gentlemen revolutionaries of 1775 were a far cry from the French revolutionaries of 1789 and an even farther cry from the Bolsheviks of 1917 and the Chinese Communists of 1949. Whereas the Communist revolutions and the French revolution were animated by an abiding passion for equality and fraternity, the American Revolution emphasized liberty and a rather narrow definition of equality. The Communist and French revolutions drew political strength from the subordinate classes, holding out the promise of the redistribution of wealth; the American revolution was led by the dominant class, which deeply feared the redistribution of wealth. The 'text' of the American revolution was about liberty, but the subtext was about the preservation of private property and the survival of what might be called the gentry and mercantile world order. The social contract in the American political imagination traces its intellectual origins to John Locke, rather than Jean-Jacques Rousseau (Locke, 1979 [1693]; Tarcov, 1984; Yoltan, 1971).

The Locke that provided intellectual sustenance to the American revolutionaries was the Locke of the Second Treatise on Government. Unlike Thomas Hobbes, Locke's original state of nature was not all against all; he presupposed a kind of understated abundance – not unlike the 'empty' American frontier. Land was held in common – not unlike the original New England village – yet individuals were free to labour and increase their products. Unlike Karl Marx, Locke considered labour to be alienable; as a form of property, labour may be bought and sold according to its market value. Land, as the primordial form of wealth, is socially and economically inert without labour. When labour is applied to commonly held land – and here is the key to Locke's social contract – it is transmuted into private property. For Marx, private property is the necessary result of alienated labour; for Locke it is the natural outcome of the individual's right to sell his or her labour. Locke believed that increase was the purpose of the social contract; the equation of individual increase with social benefit is Locke's key turn of mind (Goldwin, 1987, p. 494). According to C.B. Macpherson (1962, pp. 220-221), 'On this view his insistence that a man's labour was his own – which was the essential novelty of Locke's doctrine of property – has almost the opposite significance from that more generally attributed to it in

99

recent years; it provides the moral foundation for bourgeois appropriation.' School choice advocates who profess the cause of liberty seldom acknowledge that the social contract to which they indirectly refer also underwrites unlimited accumulation and a class state (Coleman, 1990; Arons, 1983).

It is not difficult to see how the Lockean justification of private property and individual possessiveness should find resonance with the theories of Adam Smith who provided the moral foundations for capital accumulation and is the patron saint of market-oriented reformers. Smith believed in a life that was "free, reasonable, comfortable, and tolerant" (Cropsey, 1987: 649). Like Locke, Smith had little difficulty in reconciling individual and common interests. And like Locke, Smith's social contract is not Rousseauian, bent on liberating the inner drives in the interest of a larger moral will. Smith's social contract is based on self-preservation, peaceful prosperity, and minimal state interference in the operations of the economy. The bourgeois world view as formulated by Locke and Smith is the philosophical and political basis for those who believe in the deregulation of the American public school system. To them the great Satan is the state, the great saviour is the market. The identification of private property with the public good has created a political environment conducive to school deregulation and privatization.

Current Experiments With Deregulation

There are a variety of actual and proposed market-driven school choice programs. Some of these programs are quite radical; there are market reformers who propose to dismantle public education entirely. Others are more modest; they hope to introduce market principles of organization into the existing system. An example of the former is total privatization; an example of the latter is the charter school. Undoubtedly, the coming years will see many combinations and permutations of the privatization solution. In this section we examine some of the current experiments with deregulation: these include privatization, vouchers, and charters schools. This section is largely descriptive; evidence concerning the learning outcomes of deregulation is presented somewhat later in the paper.

Privatization

Significant aspects of American public education have been privatized for decades. Textbooks and other school books are sold to school districts and schools by commercial vendors. Most public school transportation is provided by private contractors and, in many school districts, food services are privatized. Beyond these types of services, individual school districts and schools may contract with private organizations for security, special education instruction, and technological support. Beginning in the late 1980s, however, private firms such as Educational Alternatives Incorporated began to negotiate with school districts for the purpose of managing whole schools or entire school districts. Part of the incentive for this expansion of privatization was that investors were beginning to focus on the lucrative education market. The term of art on Wall Street for firms that run schools is 'educational management organization' (Toch, 1996). Presently, for-profit companies earn $30 billion a year on pre-school to high school education. While there is no reliable index about the growth of the for-profit educational market, the 'Education Industry Directory' publishes a report called *The Education Industry Report*. According to *The Report*, education is nine per cent of the Gross National Product. *The Report* identifies 25 for-profit EMOs currently traded on the stock exchange. The stock value of these companies grew 65 per cent in 1995. In February 1996, Lehman Brothers (a major brokerage house) sponsored a conference for education companies and institutional investors to look at the investment opportunities available.

Perhaps the most widely known EMO is Educational Alternatives, Inc. (EAI). This company was hired in 1992 by the Baltimore City School System to run a group of schools. In late 1995 this contract was cancelled by the city of Baltimore. This cancellation was caused in large part because EAI, in the eyes of the Baltimore City School System, failed to deliver on its promise to raise average standardized test scores. Given that EMOs evoke market efficiency as a rationale for taking over state-run schools, it is surprising that EAI spent only 48 per cent of its budget on instructional staff compared to 65 per cent in all other Baltimore public schools. EAI also had contracted with the City of Hartford, Connecticut. In this case, EAI agreed to manage the City's 24,000 student, $200 million school system for five years. The City of Hartford cancelled its contract in 1996, causing EAI to write off a $5.5 million debt. Again, the issue was EAI's inability to raise academic standards and improve student outcomes (Toch, 1996).

Another high profile EMO is the Edison Project. This company is part of Whittle Communications which made its mark in the educational for-profit sector by merchandising commercial classroom television. Originally, the Edison Project planned to open a thousand private schools to compete with public schools, but Whittle Communications ran into serious financial problems and the scope of its operations was curtailed. Currently, the Edison Project operates several schools in the Midwest and Massachusetts. It is too early to know whether the Edison schools will have any significant impact on increased learning. Other EMOs attempting to increase their market share include Alternate Public Schools, Inc, Noble Education Dynamics, Inc., Sylvian Learning Systems, and Eduventures, Inc. Almost all these companies sell educational products that are untested and there is very little systematic assessment of their effectiveness.

Vouchers

From the time of the American Revolution, arguments have been made that educational revenue streams ought to follow students and not flow directly to schools. Libertarians argue that compulsory public education is unconstitutional and represents a dangerous intrusion of the state into the educational decision making of individuals and families. Some reformers, such as John Coons & Stephen Sugarman (1992), believe that vouchers should be used as a method for obtaining educational justice by empowering the poor (see Cookson, 1994b for a justice-driven voucher plan).

Beginning with Milton Friedman (1962), market-oriented school reformers have argued that consumer accountability produces greater educational diversity and excellence than does the democratic model of school organization. Until the late 1980s this point of view was peripheral to public policy debates. In the early 1990s, however, the popularity of school vouchers rose dramatically. Today, vouchers are the educational reform policy of choice for fiscal conservatives, religious fundamentalists, market-oriented school reformers, and civil libertarians. In introducing his national voucher bill, former President Bush said, "For too long, we've shielded schools from competition, allowed our schools a damaging monopoly power over our children. And this monopoly turns students into statistics and turns parents into pawns. And it is time that we begin thinking of a system of public education in which many providers offer a marketplace of opportunities – opportunities that give all our children choices and access to the best education in the world" (Bush, 1992).

Today, there are voucher proposals in numerous states including California, Ohio, Minnesota, and Massachusetts. The only voucher proposal that has been enacted into law to date is the Milwaukee Parental Choice Program. This pilot voucher plan, the Milwaukee experiment, is the creation of an African-American assemblywoman from Milwaukee's North Side. Annette 'Polly' Williams is a former welfare mother who earned a degree at the University of Chicago while she raised her four children as a single parent. In her plan a thousand low income Milwaukee students may attend private non-sectarian schools, using public funds. Their tuition is paid for, in part or in full, by a $3,245 voucher. Funds for the private school vouchers are diverted from general school funds which would be used otherwise to support the Milwaukee public schools. This is a program for poor children and most of the private schools are small and non-élite. One of the major problems facing voucher advocates is that many private schools are not well run and are not superior to public schools. Moreover, because there is very little accountability in the voucher model, the possibilities of fraud are magnified. The principal of one of the failed private schools in Milwaukee was charged with passing $47,000 in bad cheques. Most small businesses fail within five years of starting; 80 per cent fail within ten years. Recently, the program was expanded to include religious schools, the constitutionality of which is currently being debated by the Wisconsin Supreme Court.

The primary organized opponents of vouchers are the teachers' unions and other interest groups of the 'educational establishment.' However, as the voucher movement gains momentum and becomes increasingly politicized, opposition is likely to come from defenders of public institutions who argue that the deregulation of public education presents a serious challenge to the viability of democracy.

Charter Schools

Another market-oriented reform is the charter school. According to Pricilla Wohlstetter, Richard Wenning, & Kerri Briggs:

> *Under the charter school concept, new school organizations are created by an individual charter, or written agreement, between a group of individuals who want to operate a school and the charter-granting authority – usually a school district or the state. Groups of teachers, parents, or community members, who share similar educational views and interests can organize and apply to operate a charter school. In exchange, these innovators agree to be held accountable for results and are required to measure up to the standards set forth in the school charter. Although the motivations behind charter schools are many, a primary purpose is to free schools from the public school bureaucracy and other external controls with the hopes of encouraging more innovative educational practices. (Wohlstetter, 1995, p. 332)*

The heart of the charter school concept can therefore be characterized as a basic bargain that provides autonomy but also requires accountability. Since 1991, twenty states have passed statutes permitting the establishment of charter schools. A recent federal count established that as of the beginning of 1995, 134 charter schools were founded in the United States. By the end of 1995 over 200 charter schools were established nationwide.

Charter schools are truly hybrids; they are public schools accountable to the state but rely on certain market principles to attract students. Whether or not charter schools will be more educationally effective than zoned public schools or whether the establishment of charters will lead to re-segregation and increased educational stratification cannot be determined at this time. The charter school movement is popular among legislators because it provides them with an opportunity to promote educational reform which incorporates market characteristics but safely stays within the public school structure. The charter school concept has several variants including contract schools, model schools, university supported schools, and traditional magnet schools.

Markets and High Marks: is there a relationship?

In this section, we analyze several types of data that bear on the relationship between educational markets and student learning. These data are hardly dispositive; yet, if treated as informed speculation they can be useful and serve as an empirical early warning system. Moreover, market advocates have a tendency to claim not only the moral high ground but empirical justification – a position that is highly questionable. Essentially, there are four types of choice research: controlled experimental design, comparisons between public and private schools, qualitative studies of public school choice, and program evaluations. Unfortunately, almost all the research conducted to date can be faulted for limited samples, crude measures, and questionable methodologies. Moreover, original studies that control for key variables such as sex, race, class, cognitive capacity, family educational background, and prior schooling are only now being undertaken (for an exception see Plank et al, 1993).

The earliest systematic attempt to evaluate school choice occurred in the Alum Rock, California, School District, near San Jose. This experiment was funded by the federal government as a way of determining the education and social effects a voucher plan would have on a school system. Originally, the Alum Rock experiment was to last five years and be a test case for vouchers; only the public schools of the district participated. At the peak of the experiment in 1974-1975, fourteen participating schools offered fifteen mini-programs. The Rand Corporation conducted a five-year evaluation of the experiment, but the results were inconclusive (Capell, 1978). Nevertheless, the results of the survey are interesting. Most parents at the outset of the experiment preferred their neighbourhood schools. But as families gained experience, they began to choose more distant schools. There is no indication that students' reading scores improved as a result of school choice. The Rand study revealed that 'socially advantaged families' were better informed about school choice options than other less privileged families. The Rand study was, until the late 1980s, the only empirical study of choice. By 1989, however, school choice advocates began to make many extravagant claims concerning the effects of school choice (Fliegel, 1990; Domanico, 1989). The findings, for instance, of Nancy Paulu and her colleagues who guided the proceedings at the 1989 White House Workshop on Choice and Education reveal how methodological innocence combined with political belief can distort empirical observation. When, for instance, Paulu argues that reading scores in District 4 in New York City rose dramatically after choice was implemented, she relies on hearsay, no clearly defined achievement measures, and interprets alleged associations causally (Cookson, 1994a).

The Private School 'Effect'

Market advocates argue that intrasectional comparisons concerning school choice and achievement will show few net results because it is competition that breeds excellence. To support these claims market advocates of school reform have invested a great deal of time and energy into demonstrating that private schools 'do it better' than public schools. The argument for the private school effect began in 1982 with the publication of *High School Achievement: public, Catholic and private schools compared* by James Coleman,

Thomas Hoffer, & Sally Kilgore. In this study, the authors claim that when they compared the average test scores of public and private school sophomores and seniors, there was not one subject in which public school students scored higher. After conducting a series of regression analyses the authors concluded that when the social characteristics of students were accounted for, private school students still outperformed public school students. These results have been attacked sharply, but the attacks have never received the widespread recognition of the original study (Alexander & Pallas, 1983; Goldberger & Cain, 1982).

The debate concerning the relationship of governance to student achievement was fuelled considerably when the political scientists John Chubb & Terry Moe published their book *Politics, Markets, and America's Schools* in 1990. Using the same data as the Coleman study, Chubb & Moe attempted to create an index of achievement based on the differences between sophomore and senior scores. They claimed that when they compared the effects of public and market-driven schools on student achievement, market-driven schools (i.e. private schools) outperformed public schools by a wide margin (1990, p. 214). I, among others, have written elsewhere about the methodological flaws in the Chubb & Moe approach (Cookson, 1991; Bryk & Lee, 1993). The omnibus independent variables they employ make the interpretation of results similar to random selection. But most puzzling is their confidence in drawing policy conclusions based on a regression analysis that only explains five per cent of measured student achievement (Chubb & Moe, 1990, p. 124).

Recently, sociologist and economist Richard Murnane (1994) argued that there is little evidence that private schools are more effective learning environments than public schools. He points out that scores from the 1990 National Assessment of Educational Progress (NAEP) Mathematics Assessment shows that even though private school students come from better educated families than public school students, their average achievement is only marginally better. Albert Shanker & Bella Rosenberg also examined the 1990 NAEP results and concluded, "The basic difference is that private schools can and do select their students and turn away applicants who do not meet their standards" (1992, p. 132). Since 1991 a small number of inner-city Milwaukee students have been able to opt out of the public school system by using a voucher to enrol in a private school. Political scientist John Witte is assessing the Milwaukee Plan. After comparing the achievement scores of voucher-using private school students with a control group of public school students, he found no statistical significance in their differences in achievement (1993).

A recent study by Stephen Plank et al (1993) found that students who attended choice schools did not do as well as private school students or students who were assigned to neighbourhood schools. When the authors compared the achievement scores of students in the tenth grade with those of eighth graders, the evidence indicated that choice students did not make dramatic gains when compared to students in other types of schools. Overall, these authors found that market-oriented reforms did not have a dramatic effect on student achievement.

In reviewing the findings of these studies, one should be sobered about the efficacy of market-driven school choice to produce a fair, responsive, and effective school system. Perhaps the single most powerful and compelling reality is that social class in all its complex social manifestations shapes school cultures, student outcomes, and public perceptions about a school's desirability. Many market-oriented school reformers are earnest meritocrats; they truly believe in a world where advantages should be given to the rational and smart. If this were the case, society would be very different indeed (although not necessarily better). But it is not the case. An individual's origins are the best predictor of his or her economic and social destination. Schools do very little to alter this process in the direction of fairness. The poignant and disturbing centrality of this phenomenon is underscored in a recent study by Charles Manski (1994).

Manski conducted a sophisticated computer simulation that modelled the market for schooling in a variety of situations. His model assumed that schooling outcomes are determined by three sets of actors: students, private schools, and public schools. Each student in this situation evaluates the two sectors and chooses the better option. The value that a student associates with a given sector depends on the tuition cost, the achievement attainable in the sector, and the student's intrinsic preference for the sector. In the simulation it assumes that private sector schools act competitively. Public schools choose how much revenue to spend on instruction and how much to spend for other purposes not valued by students. The market for schooling is in equilibrium if the schooling choices made by students, the tuition level chosen by private schools, and the instructional expenditures chosen by public schools are such that no actor wishes to change his or her behaviour. These variables are arrayed across alternative school finance policies applied to communities designated as poor, average, and wealthy. The simulations conducted by Manski vary the government subsidy of per student private school enrolment from $0 to $2000 to $4000.

Manski's primary result is that the type of voucher plan he models would not equalize educational opportunity across income groups. Whatever the value of the voucher, young people living in wealthy communities receive higher quality schooling than those living in poorer communities. Moreover, high income youth in a given community receive higher quality schooling on average than do low-income youth. In effect, Manski's study reveals what common sense already knows; in a society that is divided by class, voucher plans and market-driven school reforms are likely to increase class differences in opportunities for learning rather than to decrease them.

From these preliminary studies, it is evident that there is virtually no relationship between high marks, equity, and market-driven educational reform. While these findings are preliminary, policy-makers should proceed with great care in dismantling the public school system on the apparent strength of research that claims that market competition results in greater student learning.

Public Schools for the Public Good

If a market-oriented school reformer were to walk down one of America's mean streets, what would he or she see? The wreckage of a society gone mad with self-interest or an opportunity to start a small school for learning disabled students with no money? What text would provide the most penetrating analysis of America's current crisis? *The Second Treatise on Government? The Wealth of Nations?* Or the federal budget? America's poor are getting poorer not because they have failed to grasp the nuances of Locke's social contract but because they are shut out of an economy that has created a huge reserve army of the unemployed, the under-employed, and unemployable. More than one quarter of American children live in poverty ... which translates into hunger, illness, fear, and death at an early age.

Who should be the object of social policy in a society where one per cent of the population owns 56 per cent of the wealth? Does the United States suffer from concentrated poverty or concentrated wealth? I raise these issues in the context of school choice and the quasi-market because so much of what is written about educational policy has the aura of political innocence that borders on self-deception; one can reason one's way into a belief one knows to be false, recreating the belief through memory by removing from active memory the original self-deception. Cognitive self-deception is similar to selective perception, only deeper. This deep kind of self-deception, I fear, is at the heart of the market-oriented school choice movement. Instead of assessing the needs of children, these reformers give us free market rhetoric; instead of talking of breakthroughs in cognitive psychology they talk of parental choice; instead of imagining policies to help the poor help themselves, they help themselves to more resources; instead of the life of the mind, they speak of rational choice.

For over a decade the market-oriented reformers have held the policy high ground, posturing morality based on reason, dismissing ordinary 'educrates' as self interested and ineffective, building shining educational castles in the air, while 'ordinary' educators struggle with the real problems of real children. Perhaps the time has come to refocus educational policy. Perhaps the time has come to stop blaming the battered cart of education for the reckless excesses of the market donkey. Perhaps it is time for educators and others to recognize that the public schools are not responsible for the freeze in real wages, but an economy that rewards the few and punishes the many. Economic growth is not the only measure of the public good. Just as religious fundamentalism is sweeping the Islamic and Christian worlds, capitalist fundamentalism is sweeping the world economy. Based on a naive rationalism and self-interest, capitalist fundamentalism has taken the

107

Lockean social contract to an extreme that threatens to destroy civil society. By making abundance scarce, profit-seeking multi-nationalists inflict on those that are economically vulnerable physical and psychological hardships.

I suggest that the focus of educational policy shift from questions of efficiency and profitability to questions of equity and safety. Education is a strategic institution; if it loses its independence from the private sector, the public will have lost one of the few remaining public institutions that can intervene between the market and the individual. In one sense, market solutions to educational problems misdefine the purpose of education in a democracy. Creating a public trust through schools is part of a genuine social contract from which there is no escape if democracy is to survive into the next century.

References

Alexander, K. & Pallas, A. (1983) Private Schools and Public Policy: New Evidence on Cognitive Achievement in Public and Private Schools, *Sociology of Education*, 56, pp. 170-182.

Arons, S. (1983) *Compelling Belief: the culture of American schooling*. New York: McGraw Hill.

Berliner, D.C. & Biddle, B.J. (1995) *The Manufactured Crisis*. Reading: Addison-Wesley.

Bracey, G.W. (1994) The Fourth Bracey Report on the Condition of Public Education, *Phi Delta Kappan*, October, pp. 115-127.

Bryk, A.S. & Lee, V.E. (1993) Science or Policy Argument? A Rejoinder to Chubb and Moe, in E. Rasell & R. Rothstein (Ed.) *School Choice: examining the evidence*. Washington: Economic Policy Institute.

Bush, G. (1992) Remarks by the President in Ceremony for G.I. Bill Opportunity Scholarships for Children. White House Press Release.

Capell, F., Jr (1978) *A Study in Alternatives in American Education, Vol. 6: student outcomes in Alum Rock, 1974-1976*. Santa Monica: Rand Corp.

Carnegie Foundation for the Advancement of Teaching (1992) *School Choice*. Princeton: Carnegie Foundation.

Chubb, J.E. & Moe, T.M. (1990) *Politics, Markets, and American Schools*. Washington: Brookings Institution.

Clines, F.X. (1995) *New York Times*, November 3, A2, p. 22.

Coleman, J.S. (1990) *Foundations of Social Theory*. Cambridge: Harvard.

Coleman, J.S., Hoffer, T. & Kilgore, S. (1982) *High School Achievement: public, Catholic, and private schools compared*. New York: Basic Books.

Cookson, P.W., Jr (1991). Politics, markets, and America's schools: a review, *Teachers College Record*, 93, pp. 156-160.

Cookson, P.W., Jr (1992) The ideology of consumership and the coming deregulation of the public school system, in P.W. Cookson, Jr (Ed.) *The Choice Controversy*. Newbury Park: Corwin.

Cookson, P.W., Jr (1994a) *School Choice: the struggle for the soul of American education*. New Haven: Yale University Press.

Cookson, P.W., Jr (1994b) Redesigning the financing of American education to raise productivity: the case for a just voucher, in S. Hakim, P. Seidenstat & G.W. Bowman (Eds) *Privatizing Education and Educational Choice.* Westport: Praeger.

Cookson, P.W., Jr (1995) The federal commitment to educational reform, 1979-1993: from self-help to systematic reform, in W.T. Pink & G.W. Noblit (Eds) *Continuity and Contradiction: the futures of the sociology of education.* Cresskil: Hampton Press.

Cookson, P.W., Jr (1996) There is no escape clause in the social contract: the case against school vouchers, in J. Hanus & P.W. Cookson, Jr, *Choosing Schools: vouchers and American education.* Washington: American University Press.

Coons, J.E. & Sugarman, S.D. (1992) *Scholarships for Children.* Berkeley: Institute of Government Studies Press.

Cropsey, J. (1987) Adam Smith, in L. Strauss & J. Cropsey (Eds) *History of Political Philosophy.* Chicago: University of Chicago Press.

Domanico, R. (1989) *Model for Choice: a report on Manhattan's District 4.* New York: Manhattan Institute for Educational Innovation.

duPont, P.S., IV (1994) A 'G.I. Bill' for educating all children, in S. Hakim, P. Seidenstat & G.W. Bowman (Eds) *Privatizing Education and Educational Choice.* Westport: Praeger.

Elam, S. & Rose, L.C. (1995) Phi Delta Kappa/Gallup Poll of the public's attitudes toward the public schools, *Phi Delta Kappan,* September, pp. 41-56.

Fliegel, S. (1990)Creative non-compliance, in W.H. Clune & J.F. Witte (Eds) *Choice and Controversy in American Education. Vol. 2: The Practice of Choice, Decentralization and School Restructuring.* New York: Falmer.

Friedman, M. (1962) *Capitalism and Freedom.* Chicago: University of Chicago Press.

Goldberger, A.S. & Cain, G.G. (1982) The casual analysis of cognitive outcomes in the Coleman, Hoffer, and Kilgore Report, *Sociology of Education,* 55, pp. 103-122.

Goldwin, R.A. (1987) John Locke, in L. Strauss & J. Cropsey (Eds) *History of Political Philosophy.* Chicago: University of Chicago Press.

Hakim, S., Seidenstat, P. & Bowman, G.W. (Eds) (1994) *Privatizing Education and Educational Choice: concepts, plans, and experiences.* Westport: Praeger.

Henig, J.R. (1994) *Rethinking School Choice.* Princeton: Princeton University Press.

Hofstadter, R. (1966) *Anti-intellectualism in American Life.* New York: Rand.

Irwin, P.M. (1992) *Federal Education Funding Trends: a perspective.* Washington: Library of Congress.

Kemerer, F.R. (1995) The constitutionality of school vouchers, *West's Educational Law Reporter,* August, pp. 17-36.

Lieberman, M. (1989) *Privatization and Educational Choice.* New York: St Martin's.

Locke, J. [1693], (1979) *Some Thoughts Concerning Education,* (Eds) J.W. Yoltan & J.S. Yoltan. Oxford: Clarendon Press.

Macpherson, C.B. (1962) *The Political Theory of Possessive Individualism: Hobbes to Locke.* Oxford: Clarendon Press.

Manski, C. F. (1994) Systematic educational reform and social mobility: the school choice controversy, in S. Danziger, G.D. Sandefur, & D.H. Weinberg (Eds) *Confronting Poverty: prescriptions for change.* Cambridge: Harvard.

Murnane, R.J. (1994) Education and the well-being of the next generation, in S. Danziger, G.D. Sandefur, & D.H. Weinberg (Eds) *Confronting Poverty: prescriptions for change.* Cambridge: Harvard.

Persell, C.H. & Cookson, P.W., Jr (1992) *Making Sense of Society*. New York: Harper Collins.

Phillips, K. (1990) *The Politics of Rich and Poor*.New York: Random House.

Plank, S., Schiller, K.S., Schneider, B. & Coleman, J.S. (1993). Effects of choice in education, in E. Rasell & R. Rothstein (Eds) *School Choice: examining the evidence.* Washington: Economic Policy Institute.

Powell, A.G., Farrar, E. & Cohen, D.K. (1985) *The Shopping Mall High School.* Boston: Houghton Mifflin.

Rothstein, R. (1993) Myth of public school failure, *American Prospect*, 13, pp. 21-34.

Shanker, A. & Rosenberg, B. (1992). Do private schools out-perform public schools, in P.W. Cookson, Jr. (Ed.) *The Choice Controversy*. Newbury Park: Corwin.

Toch, T. (1996) Do firms run schools well? *U.S. News and World Report*, January 8, 120, pp. 46-49.

Tarcov, N. (1984) *Locke's Education for Liberty.* Chicago: University of Chicago Press.

Walford, G. (1992) Educational choice and equity in Great Britain, *Educational Policy*, 6, pp. 123-138.

Wilson, J.Q. & DiIulio, J., Jr (1995) *American Government*. Lexington, : DC Heath .

Witte, J.F. (1990) Choice and control in American education: an analytical overview, in W.H. Clune & J.F. Witte (Eds) *Choice and Control in American Education. Vol. 1: the theory of choice and control in education.* New York: Falmer.

Witte, J.F. (1993) The Milwaukee parental choice program, in E. Rasell & R. Rothstein (Eds) *School Choice: examining the evidence.* Washington: Economic Policy Institute.

Wohlstetter, P., Wenning, R. & Briggs, K.L. (1995) Charter schools in the United States: the question of autonomy, *Educational Policy*, 9, pp. 331-358.

Yoltan, J.W. (1971) *John Locke and Education.* New York: Random House.

Oxford Studies in Comparative Education, Vol. 6(1), 1996

Marketisation in Australian Schooling

SIMON MARGINSON

The Dual System of Schooling

Similar to most other Anglo-American and OECD countries, Australia has a dual system of government and private schools. Until the late 1980s the dual system consisted of a market-based private school sector and eight different government school systems, one located in each State and Territory, that were administered by government departments and fully funded from public sources. The government schools were not in competition with each other. That has now changed. Each of the State and Territory government school systems has been subjected to programmes of corporate reform and marketisation, although the extent of change has varied. In all States and Territories the government schools have been placed in competition with each other and are now partly dependent on private financing from a number of sources. Superficial observation suggests that the private and government schools have converged on the grounds of a single market in schooling. This is misleading, however. While there is considerable movement of parents between private and government schools, so that the two sectors form part of a common system of schooling and tend to affect each other, there remain important differences between private and public schools, and between the market in private schooling and the quasi-markets in government schooling (Anderson, 1992; Marginson, 1993).

The Australian schooling system is distinguished by the size of its private sector and by the weight of the private schools, especially a small number of highly élite schools, in selection into the most prestigious university faculties (Williams, 1993). In 1994, 25.5 per cent of primary students and 32.9 per cent of secondary students were enrolled outside the government school systems. With 28.5 per cent of all enrolments, Australia's private sector was one of the largest in the OECD. One reason is that unlike

111

England and New Zealand, but similar to Spain and France, the Catholic parish schools have always been separate from the government systems. A second reason is the proliferation of new private schools in the last two decades, many of them operated by minority religious groups. The private schools receive varying levels of financial support from both Commonwealth and State (regional) governments, but most private schools receive more than half of their operating funds from government sources, as well as some assistance with capital costs, and enjoy tax exemptions similar to those of their British counterparts.

Category of school	Number of schools	Number of students	Proportion of all students %
Government	7,159	2,214,939	71.5
Catholic	1,686	602,149	19.4
Anglican	120	86,184	2.8
Non-denominational private	149	48,196	1.6
Uniting church	43	39,666	1.3
Lutheran	72	19,252	0.6
Inter-denominational	45	17,001	0.5
Baptist	42	12,626	0.4
Jewish	19	8,734	0.3
Presbyterian	12	8,130	0.3
Seventh Day Adventist	71	6,560	0.2
Other Private	210	34,442	0.1
Total	9,679	3,099,380	100

Table I. School enrolments, Australia, 1994. Source: the Commonwealth Department of Employment, Education and Training, and the Australian Bureau of Statistics Catalogue Number 4221.0.

Since the beginning of direct government assistance to private schools in Australia in 1963, choice of schooling has mostly been synonymous with private schooling. In the 1960s and 1970s the application of government grants enabled the large Catholic systems to survive and modernise their science teaching, and then to employ trained lay teachers in place of members of the religious orders, whose numbers were in decline. Between 1975 and 1983 the then Liberal-National Party (conservative) national Government offered generous support to people wishing to start new private schools. New schools were funded at the maximum rate, and also received an additional 'establishment grant'. Some received capital grants. As the Government's Schools Commission (SC) put it at the time: "It ought to be possible for any group seeking to start a new school to do so on the same basis as new systemic schools have been started in recent years: that is, with low fees and relatively high subsidies from governments" (SC, 1981). Between 1977 and 1985 the number of private schools that were neither Catholic nor Anglican, many set up by small fundamentalist groups, increased from 341 to 692 (Australian Bureau of Statistics [ABS] 4221.0). The then Labor Government introduced a more restrictive new schools policy in 1985, requiring that new private schools not impact negatively on existing schools. This requirement tended to protect the government schools and Catholic systemic schools, and confined most of the new private school development to areas of demographic growth. However, on returning to office in March 1996, the Liberal-National Parties (LNP) undertook to lift the restrictions on new private schools and provide both additional capital grants and a higher initial level of funding (LNP, 1996).

In the last decade academic studies and market research have consistently indicated a high preference for private schooling, exceeding the private sectors' share of enrolments. In 1994 the regular poll commissioned by *The Age* and *The Sydney Morning Herald* asked a national sample of 1,000 people the question "If you had children, and money was no object, would you prefer them to go to a government secondary school or a non-government [i.e. private] school?" 58 per cent selected a non-government school, 32 per cent a government school and 10 per cent had no opinion. Among those people with children at government schools, 45 per cent – more than half of those who expressed an opinion – opted for the non-government sector. This shows the extent to which the private school market has become normalised as the model of all schooling in Australia. A similar poll conducted in 1986 found that of the majority who favoured private schools, almost two-thirds opted for the non-Catholic independent sector (Richards, 1994; Mills, 1986). Papadakis (1990) conducted an extensive study of attitudes to a range of services, based on a national sample of 3,507 people. He found that on all indicators, people rated private schools as superior to government schools, especially in relation to discipline, school-parent relations and in school resources (notwithstanding the continuing resource superiority of the government systems compared to the bulk of private schools). However, Papadakis also found that most respondents rated both government and private schools as "important" or "very important". Most people wanted no further expansion in the size of the private sector, with 57 per cent agreeing with the statement that "private education increases social class difference". There was a divergence between the social arrangements that people supported and their more market-oriented individual behaviour, which might vary from social preferences.

Nevertheless, the difference between the level of individual commitment to private schooling and the level of participation in private schooling suggests there is a high level of unmet demand and if government subsidies are increased, enabling private schools to either lower their fees or increase the number of places available, private school enrolments will further increase. The proportion of students in the government systems declined from 78.9 to 71.5 per cent between 1977 and 1994. Preliminary data indicate a further decline to 71.0 per cent in 1995 (ABS, 4220.0), suggesting doubts about the capacity of the government schools to retain their comprehensive character in the longer term, while the present policy settings are maintained. Ironically, while those citing a preference for private schooling often favour the elite schools, few of the parents who choose to transfer their student children from government to private schools are likely to find themselves entering the grounds of one of the leading schools. This is a small group, subject to various claims, but numbering less than 100 schools: these include the Sydney, Melbourne and Brisbane Grammars; Scotch College in Melbourne and Prince Alfred College in Adelaide, Methodist Ladies College in Melbourne and Abbotsleigh in Sydney. At all elite schools there are long waiting lists and the schools choose the families, rather than the other way around.

Corporate Reform after 1985

From the mid 1980s momentum began to build, in government and business circles, for corporate reform and marketisation in government schooling. The ground was prepared for reform by a series of well-publicised criticisms of democratic forms in school governance, on grounds that they were inherently inefficient and liable to 'producer capture' by teachers. These arguments were first raised officially by the Commonwealth's own Quality of Education Review Committee (QERC) in 1985. The QERC argued that the representative committees used in the administration of Schools Commission programmes were incompatible with sound administration:

> *The committee model was introduced as a way of ensuring active*
> *participation by interested parties in decision-making. Committees have in*
> *this sense been successful. However, there may now be too many of them for*
> *effective administration and achievement of objectives, given the number of*
> *programmes and their overlapping aims. There is, for example, no way to*
> *guarantee that any two programme committees will adopt consistent*
> *approaches when dealing with their respective but complementary programmes*
> *or will adopt approaches conducive to programme objectives. Unless*
> *committees work within focused guidelines and are subject to regular*
> *monitoring they may, by their very structure, stray easily away from the*
> *pursuit of the programme's objectives. Some rationalisation therefore, seems*
> *highly desirable. (Karmel, 1985, p. 169)*

It was significant that the QERC found the problem to be inherent in the democratic form ('by their very structure'). Over the next decade this argument was to be considerably developed. The March 1991 edition of the *Business Council Bulletin,* published by the Business Council of Australia (BCA), the leading peak council of business and industry, mounted a detailed argument against all non-corporate forms of organisation. 'Bureaucratic' organisation in schooling undermined quality because it reduced local responsibility for performance. Local managers needed greater autonomy and flexibility, with discretionary resources for inducements to staff, such as promotion or extra financial remuneration. "Management issues are at the heart of concerns about quality in public school systems", stated the BCA (BCA, 1991a). The September 1991 *Bulletin* argued against all non-market forms of organisation, whether bureaucratic or democratic. It identified two pointers towards better school organisation, which, it stated, provided "complementary and mutually reinforcing evidence" of the direction school reform should take. One was the recent history of corporate restructuring: successful companies were those that used decentralisation to achieve flexibility, responsiveness and a stronger orientation to customers. The second was research into school effectiveness. For example, Chubb & Moe (1990) had argued that mode of organisation was the crucial determinant of a school's success. Bureaucratic controls should be removed and schools made autonomous, with control over personnel and budget. The BCA saw no qualitative difference between bureaucratic and democratic models of public schooling, nor did it acknowledge the character of grass roots democracy (BCA, 1991b). The same approach was taken by government economic departments and agencies when discussing the need for corporate reform in schooling (for example Clare & Johnston, 1993).

Beginning with the partial decentralisation of the New South Wales (NSW) system in 1988, over the next half decade the eight State and Territory systems were each subject to reform. Lingard et al (1995) summarise the 'ministerialisation' of the government education systems in Australia, whereby reforming ministers of education asserted control by dismantling or restructuring the programme departments responsible for education. The new agenda was implemented by generic system managers drawn from elsewhere in the public service or the private sector: by 1992 not a single one of the education departments in Australia was headed by an educator who had come up through the system in a conventional way. The substance of the reforms was similar to those in New Zealand, and reflected the prevailing market liberal assumptions concerning public sector reform. The existing departmental structures were radically restructured or abolished and replaced by new formations. Actual models varied, reflecting the different history of the States, but there was a convergence around the common corporate model of a strong centre, joined to local autonomy that was "steered from the distance". In NSW new regional structures were created as instruments of a modernised system of central control; in Western Australia (WA) the old regional structures were abolished because they were impediments to the new central control. In all cases smaller, streamlined head offices were established with a stronger hold on the now more autonomous schools (Porter et al, 1993).

In most systems, schools received greater control over their financial resources, while corporate systems of accountability were introduced, facilitated by computerised accounting which standardised both school-level management and reporting to the centre (Hill & Russell, 1994, p. 26). For example, in Western Australia part of government funding was devolved to schools without detailed specifications as to its use, while the schools were made accountable for performance against centrally established standards and goals. Those systems where zoning still applied were dezoned, and competition for enrolments was established between the neighbouring government schools. In some States, such as NSW, the government encouraged the emergence of academically selective government schools and schools competing for niche markets, such as those specialising in music or languages. School councils were introduced in NSW, but everywhere school council responsibilities were changed, so that the councils were focused more on matters of resource management, staffing and fundraising; and rather less on curriculum matters. Teacher representation on school councils was restricted. In all systems, principals began to be described and treated as school managers, with a dual responsibility to school council and government. In some States there was a partial decentralisation of staff appointments, especially of non-teaching staff. In all systems schools were now encouraged to raise their own funding to supplement government grants. This was a radical change from traditional norms, but in all systems government funding was by now tightly restrained, or was reducing in real terms, and in many schools a mixed public/private funding regime seemed to offer a partial way out of their funding difficulties.

The new systems were quasi-markets in which performance measurement and competition were established, schools were run by quasi-corporations and student fees and other forms of private income played a growing role. At the same time, in the legal sense government schools remained within the public domain, the majority of funds continued to be provided by governments, and central authority could still be exerted at will. "The freedom which schools have is more to do with means than ends" (Knight et al, 1993). Governments continued to shape the character of government schooling, so that variations occurred only within the narrow band of officially sanctioned possibilities. There continued to be less diversity in government schooling than in the private sector. As in Britain, devolution was accompanied by a partial centralisation and standardisation of curricula. Although negotiations over national curriculum frameworks broke down (Lingard et al, 1995), by 1995 all States and Territories except Tasmania had introduced standardised testing. Most of the systems tested students in both Years 3 and 5 of primary school.

The outcome was a new politics of schooling in which the older relations of power were preserved. The epicentre of political power did not change but the responsibility was transferred from the centre downwards to school communities. Devolution and market competition weakened the scope for system-wide political pressures from below, especially pressures directed at increasing resources across the board, or re-reforming the system itself. The solidarity of local communities became a tool of system management and was ranged against neighbouring communities. Once established, these competing corporations were naturalised; and alternative, more co-operative forms of system organisation faded from view. Meanwhile the centre's role in system setting became strangely opaque, an unseen presence widely felt but scarcely to be expressed, a technical matter of system management, no longer subjected to political decision and public debate. Arguably, since the beginning of the 1990s the influence of the system-wide organisations of parents and teachers has been reduced, in every State and Territory. Parent and teacher organisations have yet to devise strategies and tactics appropriate to the new environment.

At the same time, there are some signs that the course of market reform has further to run. In 1993 the Commonwealth's Economic Planning Advisory Council (EPAC) suggested that if devolution "does not succeed in producing the necessary responsiveness and accountability" perhaps school communities should be allowed to "opt out of the central system altogether". Government funding could be linked to "implementation of core curriculum subjects, the achievement of specified standards in external examination of students and/or the certification of the educational approach used within a school" (Clare & Johnston, 1993). In 1995 the Department of Employment, Education and Training (DEET) floated the possible break-up of the government systems into smaller units, or "contracting of parts of the delivery system to partly or wholly privatised providers" (DEET, 1995). The presence of Liberal-National Party governments in five of the six States, and at the national level, brings these kinds of possibilities closer than before.

Victoria: schools of the future

The most far-reaching reforms were introduced in the State of Victoria, where the changes have been on the scale of those implemented in Britain and New Zealand. In Victorian Government schooling there was a strong if uneven tradition of local democratic forms. Devolution developed initially as a means of modifying, or escaping from, central control; and was influenced by the New Left and its effects in teaching. In some Victorian secondary schools leadership was supplied by an elected staff executive rather than the principal. In the second half of the 1980s the emphasis began to shift in favour of corporate forms of devolution, and the modernisation of central control rather than its negation. In 1986 the then Labor Government floated proposals for full-scale devolution of both curriculum and resource allocation, *Taking schools into the 1990s* (Government of Victoria [VG], 1986). This was withdrawn after opposition from teacher and parent organisations (Watkins

& Blackmore, 1993), but the new Liberal-National Party Government, which came to power in October 1992, promised to revive devolution in the context of a more market-oriented government school system.

The reforms in Victorian Government schooling were preceded by dramatic resource reductions which structured the purpose and the character of the reforms from the beginning. In its first fifteen months 230 government schools were closed, spending was cut by over \$AUD300 million and 8200 teaching positions were abolished, almost one teacher in every five. Student-staff ratios and class sizes rose dramatically. For example, between 1992 and 1994 the proportion of junior primary and infant classes with over 25 students rose from 35 to 72 per cent (Australian Education Union [AEU], 1994). The 568 special teaching positions allocated for schools experiencing socio-economic disadvantage were abolished, half of the specialist positions in migrant English were abolished and as a result there was some redistribution of net staffing resources in favour of middle class districts and away from non-Anglo communities (McMurdo & Peace, 1993). In the midst of debate about the resource reductions, the Government announced its 'Schools of the Future' programme in 1993.

Schools of the Future began on a pilot basis. Publicly, the main emphasis lay on the devolution aspect. "The aim is for each School of the Future to have complete control over its financial resources and to have the capacity to plan how these resources will be used across the full range of staff, services, equipment and supplies', according to the Government" (VG, 1993). Authority for the management of schools was devolved to school councils. Before the Schools of the Future programme was introduced, school councils in Victoria had operated as collaborative policy making bodies for teachers and parents, and the focus was on the educational programme. Now the focus was shifted to the management of resources and personnel, and less attention was given to educational programmes, especially core activities. To head off 'producer capture' by teachers no more than one third of each council were allowed to be DSE employees. School councils were made responsible for the policies of the school, the employment of staff, the approval and if necessary variation of the school budget, and the selection of the principal, although required to include a representative of the DSE on the panel. It was intended that eventually schools would select all their own staff, although these would continue to be DSE employed. However, although councils could negotiate their own contracts the minister retained the power to make any order in relation to those contracts; and the minister retained the power to direct councils while no longer legally liable for their actions. In practice management of the school rested not with the council but with the principal, who could shape the agenda and judgements of the council. "The principal will be responsible and accountable for curriculum leadership, resource and personnel management, and school organisation" (VG, 1993). The principal was accountable to both council and DSE, but in the case of conflict between the two, the tie to the DSE was determining:

through each principal the Government exercised an unstated but effective control over school management decisions.

As in New Zealand, the school council and the principal were required to develop a school 'charter' as the basis of a limited life 'contract' between the school and its funding agency, the DSE. Through the charter agreement, the Government undertook to supply the school with a level of funding based on the school's 'profile', derived from the size and composition of its student body, its physical resources, geographical and sociological factors affecting the school, and the curriculum and services it undertook to provide. Through negotiations over the agreements, the Government was able to influence the development of school programmes, shape the division of labour between schools, and vary resource levels significantly between schools, while evading a public process of planning in which all local schools would be considered together. With schools dezoned, and funding largely determined by the level of enrolments, schools were placed in competition for Government resources, for parental finance in the form of quasi-compulsory fees, levies and donations; and for sponsorship and community support for purposes consistent with the school charter (Kenway, 1993). Schools could provide educational services on the basis of contracts with private providers or other schools, inviting commercial development, and were encouraged to contract out not only in-school services such as cleaning, but also some of their educational activities.

By the beginning of 1995 the programme had been established in the majority of Victoria's 1,700 government schools. All Schools of the Future were subject to charter arrangements. Each controlled budgets constituting more than 90 per cent of expenditure, with principals having the authority to select staff (Caldwell, 1994).

Schools of the Future set out to reconstruct three basic relationships that constituted the system of schooling. The first relationship was that between the school and its community: parents were treated as 'consumers' of the individual school rather than citizen-members of a common system of schools, in which everyone had an interest in everyone else's welfare. The second relationship was that between the school and other schools. For the first time, government schools were competing directly with each other so that, as in all schooling markets, the success of one school was the failure of another. The medium for this competition was the struggle for enrolments and funding. The main signifier of a school's competitiveness, the educational equivalent of its share price or its profit result, was the performance of its students in examinations and standardised tests. The third relationship was that between schools and the government: the programme devolved managerial responsibilities and some of the responsibilities for funding and staffing to the local school level, but control over educational policy was more firmly re-centred under government control. At the same time individual schools, rather than the system as a whole, were now responsible for educational and social outcomes and system organisation had been depoliticised, naturalising the quasi-market. Caldwell describes it as "administrative decentralisation rather than political decentralisation". The centre remained the "strategic core", providing the system framework of "mission, strategy, policy, priority and accountability". The local units gained only "the capacity for management within a centrally determined framework" (Caldwell, 1993). Administrative decentralisation could be over-determined at any time, or even reversed altogether at whim. In curriculum matters, the hold of the centre was mostly tighter than before. To Seddon (1994) the opportunity to "be involved in the determination of what the choices options are to be" is crucial to effective participation. But the Schools of the Future programme established "unequal power relations" in which the central authority defined what constitutes "quality" education and imposed that definition on both its own employees and their "customers". Critical questions about the scope of education, about "what is possible and desirable for an education system to achieve", and the pattern of schooling, "the contexts, conditions and resources within which schools operate" remained centrally determined.

The reforms in Victoria have yet to be subject to the kind of close empirical scrutiny carried out in the Smithfield project in New Zealand (Lauder et al, 1994) and the work of Whitty, Edwards and others in the UK (Edwards & Whitty, 1994). However, one important statistic has already emerged: the trajectory of retention rates since the reforms were introduced. Total retention to Year 12 of secondary schooling in Victoria has fallen from 81.1 per cent in 1992 to 75.0 per cent in 1995 (ABS, 4221.0). Over the 1992 to 1995 period national Year 12 retention also fell, but at a slower rate. It is likely that the retreat from education in Victoria has been affected by Government policies, but it is difficult to distinguish the effects of corporate reform in schooling from the reduction in resources, and other influences such as the impact of the early 1990s recession on propensity to enrol.

Fees, Fundraising and Commercialisation

With government schools in Australia now organised as corporate institutions in competition with each other and partly responsible for raising their own resources, there has been a marked increase in the proportion of funds obtained from fees and commercial sponsorship. Evidence is beginning to emerge that, as could be expected, the capacity to raise non-government income, particularly from school parents and local business firms, is differentiated along socio-economic lines. The increased dependence on private funds is creating the basis for a growing resource disparity between schools in working-class zones and those in middle-class zones.

In the early 1990s the long tradition of "free, compulsory and secular" in Australian government schools was overturned. Fees became widespread in government schools, although they were not quite compulsory or universal (DEET, 1995). In most States the schools were able to specify their own standard fees within a government-determined upper limit. In South Australia fees ranged from $90 to $300 per year. Victorian primary schools charged a standard $40 to $75, and secondary schools from $200 to $300 per year. A 1995 study of 50 schools in several States and Territories by the University of NSW Public Sector Research Centre (PSRC), found that a general service fee was charged in all schools and it was paid by just over four-fifths of parents. The average general fees were $56 per student in primary school and $130 in secondary schools. In 44 of the schools in the study principals stated that fees were an important source of income. Many saw fees as crucial to normal operations and predicted that fee charging would increase in future (Howard & Coulter, 1995).

As a result of these developments 'free education' began to be redefined, so that it referred to a narrowing core of 'free tuition' based on free teacher time. Outside this core, schools claimed the right to charge for a range of 'incidental costs' including course materials, textbooks, use of school computers, access to libraries, sports equipment, school visits reckoned part of the learning programme, and extra tuition outside school hours. Some teaching positions were funded from fees. There were cases of enrolment levies, building levies and even report fees. This meant that the socio-economic position of families could determine the range of educational options available to their children. For example, in NSW fees were charged for elective subjects such as computer science, home science, technical drawing and languages, excluding certain students from poorer families. In the case of fees levied on everyone, some families secured exemptions on socio-economic grounds, but with so many specific charges for different services it was necessary to obtain multiple exemptions, exacerbating stigmatisation:

> *Students have had school prizes withheld and attendance at end of year graduation ceremonies refused because of non-payment towards the cost, and letters soliciting donations or contributions from parents may contain open or veiled threats ... that individual children will be disadvantaged if the requested payment is not forthcoming (Ludbrook, 1995).*

"In some cases, teachers have called the child to the front of the class to be told that they can't do the subject because they haven't paid fees" (Totaro, 1991). In 1994 the executive director of resources and services in the WA education department wrote to schools authorising debt collectors to secure fees (Department of Employment, Education and Training [DEET], 1995).

A 1995 Monash University study of budgets from 122 Victorian schools discovered that the government schools in that State now survive 'to a large extent on the goodwill and support of the local communities'. On average almost one third of the operating expenses of schools in the study, exclusive of funded staff salaries and capital costs, were paid from the schools' own fundraising. Parents contributed an average $165 per student per year. There was a marked variation between the different socio-economic zones, with contributions ranging from $19 to $522 per student. Some schools covered more than half of their operating expenses by fundraising, while others paid for less than 10 per cent in this manner. Surry Hills primary school, in an affluent zone, raised $107,000 in 1994 by an art and craft show, voluntary parental contributions and a trust fund. The money was directed into computers and language teaching. In contrast, schools in working-class areas declared a school fair a major success if it raised $1,000 or more (Rollins, 1995).

In the study of fifty schools Howard & Coulter (1995) found that the average income from fees was $43 per student in primary schools and $117 in secondary schools, while the average income from fundraising was $49 in primary and $41 in secondary. Rural schools received rather more than average in fundraising and less than average in fees. In total fees, sponsorship and private fundraising paid for 27 per cent of operating costs. All 50 principals stated that their schools were involved in fundraising activities, 46 schools had a formal fundraising apparatus and 40 stated that fundraising was essential to maintaining what were perceived as the core educational services, especially in computing. A very wide range of fundraising activities were carried out. Few of these activities bore any relation to the teaching and learning programme of the schools concerned. The most commonly cited activities, named by 30 per cent of schools or more, were provision of the school canteen, the hire of facilities, food drives (items such as chocolates, cakes, pizzas and wine), raffles, student dances, fun runs and fetes. Two-thirds of the schools used fundraising income for computer hardware or software, and more than half for teaching and curriculum resources, especially in reading, science and maths. One third of schools used the money for building extensions or maintenance, and another third for library equipment or books. Most principals in the study made unsolicited comments about the inadequacy of government funding. "Many comments were strident in tone". One principal stated that:

> *Schools previously could provide quality programmes and resources with funds from school-generated fundraising. This is no longer the case and the funds only help in achieving a basic education service. (Quoted in Howard & Coulter, 1995, p. 17.)*

Several of the principals stated that the growing reliance on fundraising was exacerbating the resource differences between schools.

In the late 1980s and early 1990s the State and Territory governments withdrew the existing prohibitions banning company promotion within school grounds, and thus preventing the receipt of income from commercial sponsorship. As Kenway et al (1995) note in their examination of commercial sponsorship, the line between philanthropy and marketing is often blurred. Companies normally link sponsorship to the promotion of their products, for example by tying donations to consumption of a certain volume of the company's product. In the case of companies that manufacture addictive products such as fast foods, chocolates and soft drinks, the objective is to secure students as lifelong consumers of their products. Howard & Coulter found that sponsorship was less important than fees or fundraising, but 39 of the 50 schools had sponsorship arrangements. Kenway et al cite a number of examples of commercial sponsorship, including:

> *The School Bag Company, the Mars Sports Equipment Programme, the MeadowLea/Harper Collins Barcodes for Books promotion, and the Pizza Hut's Book It and Sport It! Incentive Programs. For example the School Sample Bag Company provides schools with 'show bags' containing a small selection of 'nutritious products', a copy of WHO magazine, various 'educational' competitions, some advertising brochures and a marketing questionnaire for parents. Bags are provided free of charge to schools which receive a commission for each bag that a child takes home and which use the bags in a variety of ways, e.g.. rewards for students. Manufacturers pay for the opportunity to have their product(s) included in the bag. (Kenway et al, 1995, p. 89)*

Howard & Coulter document a number of sponsorship arrangements, many common to more than one State school system. In conjunction with sponsorship and company promotion in schools, Apple marketed an extensive range of curriculum software. Coles supermarkets combined with Apple to provide computer equipment in exchange for a specified minimum level of spending at Coles. In Victoria, Cygnus computers even secured the use of its logo in a primary school's main signage, in exchange for assistance with the school's computer systems and software, and computer tuition for parents and teachers. The Commonwealth Bank, hoping to build a lifetime clientele, provided schools with 25c for every banking transaction. Another bank, Westpac, conducted a mathematics competition. Tambrand, manufacturers of Tampax tampons, provided schools with nurses who talked about menstruation, provided information on the company's products, and donated samples. Heinz provided netball and volleyball equipment in exchange for soup labels. Fruitbox, Tip Top bread, Milo and Hungry Jacks also promoted sport. Pizza Hut 'Sport it' and 'Book It' competitions provided students with vouchers requiring students to eat at Pizza Hut. In NSW Smith's snackfoods provided $50 worth of books, computer software or sporting equipment to the school for every $1,000 of Smith Snackfoods bought. More than 1,000 schools reached sponsorship deals with Mars: schools collecting 20,000 chocolate wrappers produced by the company received $1,000 worth of sporting equipment. The ubiquitous hamburger manufacturer McDonalds was the company most active in sponsorship and promotion in schools. In NSW McDonalds provided teacher of the month and student of the month awards and promoted junior basketball. One in five schools in NSW ran a 'McHappy Hour', a one-hour period at a specified McDonalds when 10 per cent of drivethru and counter sales from the students and school community were given to the school. Some teachers acted as 'celebrity servers' during these 'McHappy Hours' (Powell, 1993). McDonalds also reached a three-year agreement on school sports sponsorship with the NSW education department. The department caused an outcry when in a letter to schools it asked them to involve McDonalds in carnivals, speech nights, fundraising activities and the school magazine.

The schools had little choice but to look at every possible opportunity for income, so that the corporations were able to set the terms of the relationship. With growing competition between schools for the sponsor dollar, in Victoria a consultancy was established to advise them on strategies. Despite the existence of State guidelines for dealing with sponsors 'there is little or no monitoring of these type of activities where schools engage directly with private organisations' (Howard & Coulter, 1995). In effect, government education provided an administrative framework which McDonalds, Mars, Apple and others exploited as a system-market. The start-up costs of this form of company marketing – the infrastructure and administrative systems that sustained the student population for marketing purposes, and the techniques whereby this population was assembled at regular intervals – were free of charge. The State departments placed a low price on these lucrative system level benefits, and individual schools were in no position to bargain over their value.

Conclusion

In 1995 DEET suggested that the normalisation of fees in government schools meant that from the point of view of parents, the two parts of the dual system of schooling were converging: "the choice is not between a no fee government school and a fee-charging non-government school but a general question of parental perceptions of affordability and value among all schools" (DEET 1995). Government and private schools now share a corporate structure, with the principal as manager and the council as a quasi board of directors, and schools of both types are engaged in marketing, public relations and fundraising. However, while market relations have been extended to government schools as well as private schools, and inter-school competition has been made universal, this is not a singular market. It is segmented as schooling markets always are, and one of the segmentations falls along the government-private school divide. Nor has it abolished the legal, political and status distinctions between the school sectors.

First, private schools are affected by government policies, but the conditions governing government funding are light, university entrance requirements exercise a more profound influence on teaching and learning in private schools than do governments and private schools govern themselves. They are accountable first of all to their own communities. In the marketised government schools, the situation is different. At bottom they are accountable first of all to governments and always subject to them. Governments continue to tinker with the devolved systems they had created. Schools had been let to their communities, rather than ceded to them. Second, by adopting the forms of a market the government systems have not obtained the same status as the elite private schools, or the Catholic systems. Instead they have been confirmed in their 'inferiority' on the basis of market comparisons, while giving away claims to an alternative rationale and basis for intersectoral comparison, one grounded in their own positive role as comprehensive institutions. The outcome of market reform in the government system is that there are now two different market sectors, within one common and singular competition in schooling. Schools in Australia are now segmented between two kinds of school. First, there are the schools that are exclusive to varying degrees, schools that choose parents rather than the other way around. These are mostly private schools, but there are also some 'over-subscribed' government schools as well, especially in NSW. Second, there are schools that are freely accessible to parental choice, and thus condemned to inferiority in their social standing and educational resources. These schools are disproportionately located in the government systems. A conclusive body of evidence is not yet available, but the evidence so far indicates that the gap between these two kinds of school is widening significantly. It may be that a century of policies designed to maintain resource equality across the government systems has now ended. It is a sign of the times that not one State or Territory government is monitoring the trends in intra-system resource distribution.

References

Anderson, D. (1992) The interaction of public and private school systems, *Australian Journal of Education*, 36, pp. 213-236.

Australian Bureau of Statistics (4220.0) *National Schools Collection, Australia, Preliminary.* Canberra: ABS.

Australian Bureau of Statistics (4221.0) *National Schools Collection, Australia.* Canberra: ABS.

Australian Education Union (1994) *National Survey of Conditions in Schools.* Melbourne: AEU.

Business Council of Australia (1991a) Management of public education systems: a critical issue for quality, *Business Council Bulletin*, March, pp. 6-7.

Business Council of Australia (BCA) (1991b) Managing public education systems for improved performance, *Business Council Bulletin*, September, pp. 12-16.

Caldwell, B. (1993) Decentralising the management of Australia's schools, seminar paper to the National Industry Education Forum. Melbourne: University of Melbourne.

Caldwell, B. (1994) Resourcing the transformation of school education, inaugural professorial lecture. Melbourne: University of Melbourne.

Chubb, J. & Moe, T. (1990) *Politics, Markets and America's Schools.* Washington: Brookings Institution.

Clarke, R. & Johnston, K. (1993) *Education and Training in the 1990s.* Economic Planning Advisory Council Background Paper No. 31. Canberra: Australian Government Publishing Service.

Department of Employment, Education and Training (1995) *Discussion Paper: review of new schools policy*. Canberra: Australian Government Publishing Service.

Edwards, T. & Whitty, G. (1994) Parental choice and school autonomy: the English experience, *Unicorn*, 20, pp. 25-34.

Hill, P. & V.J. Russell (1994) *Resource Levels for Government Primary Schools*. Report prepared as part of a review by the Commonwealth government of recurrent funding for government primary schools. Melbourne: University of Melbourne.

Howard, M. & Coulter, J. (1995) *Scrounging to Meet the Shortfall: fees, fundraising and sponsorship in government schools*. Report prepared for the Public Sector Research Centre (PSRC) at the University of New South Wales. Sydney: PSRC.

Karmel, P., Committee Chair (1985), *Quality of Education in Australia*. Report of the Quality of Education Review Committee. Canberra: Australian Government Publishing Service.

Kenway, J. with Bigum, C. & Fitzclarence, L. (1993) Marketing education in the postmodern age, in J. Kenway (Ed.) *Marketing Education: some critical issues*. Geelong: Deakin University.

Kenway, J. with Bigum, C. & Fitzclarence, L., with Collier, J., & Tregenza, K. (1995) *New Education in New Times* (mimeo). Geelong: Deakin University.

Knight, J., Lingard, B. & Porter, P. (1993) Restructuring schooling towards the 1990s, in B. Lingard, J. Knight & P. Porter (Eds) *Schooling Reform in Hard Times*. London: Falmer.

Lauder, H., Hughes, D., Waslander, S., Thrupp, M., McGlinn, J., Newton, S. & Dupuis, A. (1994) *The Creation of Market Competition for Education in New Zealand*. First report to the Ministry of Education. Wellington: Victoria University.

Liberal and National Parties (1996) *Schools and TAFE*. Federal election policies. Melbourne: LNP.

Lingard, B., Porter, P., Bartlett, L. & Knight, J. (1995) Federal/State mediations in the Australian national education agenda: from the AEC to MCEETYA, 1987-93, *Australian Journal of Education*, 39, pp. 41-66.

Ludbrook, R. (1995) The law report: free education, rhetoric or reality? *Education Alternatives*, 4(2), p. 3; p. 11.

Marginson, S. (1992) Productivity in the nonmarket services: issues and problems, *Labour Economics and Productivity*, 4, pp. 53-71.

Marginson, S, (1993) *Education and Public Policy in Australia*. Melbourne: Cambridge University Press.

Marginson, S. (forthcoming) For All of Us? Government, Education and Citizenship in Australia since 1960.

McMurdo, G. & Peace, M. (1993) Whatever happened to special needs? *VSTA News*, 10 February.

Mills, S. (1986) Most Australians prefer private schools for their children: poll, *The Age*, 9 September.

Papadakis, E. (1990) Attitudes to state and private welfare: analysis of results from a national survey, *SPRC Reports and Proceedings*, 88. Sydney: Social Policy Research Centre, University of New South Wales, Australia.

Porter, P., Knight, J. & Lingard, B. (1993) The efficient corporate state: labor restructuring for better schools in Western Australia, in B. Lingard, J. Knight & P. Porter (Eds) *Schooling Reform in Hard Times*. London: Falmer.

Powell, S. (1993) Teachers tell schools: no McFeasting for funds, *The Sydney Morning Herald*, 21 September.

Richards, C. (1994) Government schools fail confidence test, *The Age*, 2 August 1994.

Rollins, A. (1995) Families pay a high price for education, *The Sunday Age*, 15 October.

Schools Commision, (SC), Commonwealth of Australia (1978) *Report for the Triennium 1979-81*. Canberra: Australian Government Publishing Service.

Schools Commision, (SC), Commonwealth of Australia (1981) *Report for the Triennium 1982-84*. Canberra: Australian Government Publishing Service.

Seddon, T. (1994) *Schools of the Future and Schools of the Past: assessing the institutional context of decentralised school management* (mimeo). Melbourne: Monash University.

Susskind, A. (1991) Under siege but fighting back, *The Sydney Morning Herald*, 26 March.

Totaro, P. (1991) The quiet revolution in education, *The Sydney Morning Herald*, 27 June.

Victoria, Government of, (VG) (1986) *Taking Schools into the 1990s*. Melbourne: Victorian Ministry of Education.

Victoria, Government of, (VG) (1993) *Schools of the Future: preliminary paper*. Melbourne: Directorate of School Education.

Watkins, P. & Blackmore, J. (1993) The development of representative committee in Victorian schools: new structures in the democratisation of educational administration?, in B. Lingard, J. Knight & P. Porter (Eds) *Schooling Reform in Hard Times*. London: Falmer.

Williams, T. (1993) *Higher Education in the 1980s*. Melbourne: Australian Council for Educational Research.

Oxford Studies in Comparative Education, Vol. 6(1), 1996

School Choice and the Quasi-market in New Zealand: 'Tomorrow's Schools' today

LIZ GORDON

Prior to the Tomorrow's Schools reforms of 1989, New Zealand had one of the most centralised and social democratic systems of education in the world. Based on the comprehensive ideal which was so elusive in the United Kingdom, New Zealand's schools promised equality of opportunity to all children regardless of who they were, where they lived and "to the fullest extent of their powers", to use the words of Peter Fraser, Minister of Education in the pre-war Labour Government. Although the indigenous Maori people suffered the same fate as minority cultures in other countries, performing far worse than Europeans in national examinations, New Zealand scored consistently at the top of international ratings of literacy (Elley, 1994), not because the best were better than the world's best, but because there was a narrower range of abilities than in many other countries; with the poorest performers scoring significantly better than the world's worst.[1]

New Zealand has always had a very centralised system of state education. The Department of Education, prior to 1989, was a large multifaceted organisation which developed collegial relations within the sector; more formally with teacher unions and schools, and less so with a whole range of consultants, community contacts and individuals. Regional education organisations were represented by Education Boards (at the primary level) and Secondary School Boards. They had no relationship with local authorities and no direct political party input. Their power was strictly circumscribed and their role primarily to distribute a very limited amount of resources, although there was the possibility of input into national policy-making.

The basis of post-war education in New Zealand was *comparable quality* of schooling. It was assumed that wherever people lived they would have access to a school offering the same range of opportunities as any other school. It was the role of the Department of Education to maintain this comparability, which led to highly interventionist (and often paternalistic) policy forms. This system, and the understandings and processes which underpinned it, was swept away in the reforms of 1989. Key aspects of these reforms were:

- the abolition of the Department of Education, and its replacement with a smaller, policy-focused Ministry plus four other stand-alone agencies covering accountability, qualifications and assessment, special education and training;
- the abolition of all regional bodies; regional functions were mainly devolved to schools, and remaining elements privatised;
- new Boards of Trustees set up to govern each school, to consist of parents elected by parents, a staff representative, the school Principal and, in secondary schools, a student representative.

This new system could be read in two ways, and indeed there were vociferous debates in the early years of reform over what kind of system was being set up. On the one hand, the influence of neo-liberal elements was evident in the separation of policy from operations, aspects of contestability and privatisation, and a new emphasis on parental choice (Hood, 1995; Lauder et al, 1994). On the other hand, the system looked like a real devolution of power from the central state to parents and schools, following the 'community empowerment' model being proclaimed at the time by the Labour Government (Gordon, 1992).

The Tomorrow's Schools reforms are now into their seventh year of operation, with the tension between 'market' and 'community' goals (Wilson, 1991) unequivocally resolved in favour of the market. Donald Hirsch (1995) notes of New Zealand:

> *This is the only country that I know of that has taken the radical step of abolishing its education system. Rather than a system, it has a series of virtually autonomous providers of education. (1995, p. 6)*

Controlled by a series of state agencies which nevertheless abhor 'intervention' (at least in theory), with no regional services to assist with planning or school operations, New Zealand schools are essentially left alone to work through, adapt to and influence market forces, while the "small, strong state" (Gamble, 1988) continues its withdrawal. This system, today, is the subject of this paper.

An Education Quasi-market

The term 'quasi-market' (Le Grand, 1991; Glennerster, 1991) was coined to refer to a particular policy pattern evident in the service agencies of the state (especially health, education and social security), in those western countries which have a tradition of Keynesian forms of state provision, but aspirations towards a neo-liberal non-interventionist state. The quasi-market is essentially a 'halfway house' between interventionist and non-interventionist state forms, although it is in itself relatively stable. The reason for the development of quasi-market forms is best expressed in Michael Pusey's (1991) analysis of economic rationalism in the Australian context. He points out that whilst the central control agencies of the state (especially the finance agencies), and the state-owned trading entities, were in a position to adapt readily to the demands of neo-liberal reform, through administrative reorganisation or privatisation, the service agencies were not. The development of quasi-markets was a response to this problem.

The reason that the service agencies, and especially education, were not adaptable to neo-liberal reform lies in their very nature. A clue to this, for example, was the New Zealand Treasury's (1987) blueprint for educational reform, where the authors questioned whether it was justifiable for a state even to require compulsory education of its population. From a classical neo-liberal position (Nozick, 1974; Hayek, 1991), such provision is not justifiable; it is an unwarranted and sinister intrusion into individual freedom. Therefore, any state with neo-liberal aspirations which wants (or needs) to hold to compulsory education is forced into an insoluble contradiction. If the state requires people to attend school, then it must at least fund schools and probably provide them too. The problem, for Western states, was how to ensure compulsion in a way which upheld neo-liberal imperatives of non-intervention and market forces. The quasi-market was the (partial) solution. The state would largely continue to fund, and, to a lesser extent provide, services, but as far as possible the system would be subjected to choice and competition, guided by the 'hidden hand' of market forces rather than a state bureaucracy. A crisis of political legitimation (Dale, 1989) would be averted, whilst education would be marketised.

For Le Grand, the development of quasi-market policy patterns in the British welfare context encompasses two central elements. The first is the separation of funding from provision, with the state becoming essentially a *funder* of welfare services, "purchasing services from a variety of private, voluntary and public providers, all operating in competition with one another" (1991, p. 1257). Secondly, funding is provided in different ways, cutting out the bureaucratic machinery in favour of direct grants, either to users (in education, a voucher scheme) or their agents. Bartlett (1993, p. 125) notes that the aim of quasi-market educational reform has been:

> ... *to attempt to bring about an improvement in the quality of educational provision by creating a system in which high-quality provision is financially rewarded. The idea has been that such a system of rewards works best when decision-making is decentralised ... This is the essence of the new quasi-market system, in that the size of the school's budget is linked to the numbers of pupils it can attract.*

With the exception of teacher salaries, which are largely paid directly by the central state,[2] and some programmes of deferred maintenance and capital development, schools in New Zealand have complete control over their budgets, and funding may be spent as Boards of Trustees wish. Schools may buy services from the private sector, borrow money and fund capital development, although certain things are still subject to Ministerial approval. It is the level of autonomy that schools have which determines the extent to which a quasi-market environment can be developed in education, and New Zealand schools have more autonomy than those in virtually any other country (OECD, 1994).

The market is underpinned by a particular conception of 'parental choice'. As in England, the particular model of choice applied to New Zealand schools is that which Dale & Ozga call 'exit', over the more participatory model of choice as 'voice', which encourages people to stay in institutions and make changes from within. According to Dale & Ozga (1993, p. 76): "exit is an individualistic, economic response, while voice is a participatory, political response". This approach to choice encourages a highly mobile population, based on a core of active 'choosers'. The 'exit' model of choice is a necessary concomitant to the quasi-market, because it emphasises the *portable* nature of the funds brought by the student, and the fact that they can be taken away at any time.

Schools are funded almost entirely on the basis of student numbers. In order to maintain or improve funding levels, schools must thus attract students in similar or increased numbers, year after year. The effect of losing students is to lose operational funding and staff. Thus a primary driving force of schools in the quasi-market environment is maintaining and improving student numbers. Given that this was not a major concern in the past, a quite fundamental shift has occurred in school priorities in the current policy environment.

School Choice: the quasi-market in operation

Over the past decade, New Zealand has had the fastest growing gap between the incomes of the richest and poorest amongst a range of similar countries (Joseph Rowntree Foundation, 1995; Hills, 1995). There is a growing tendency towards polarisation between social groups (Saunders, 1994). Not surprisingly, a key feature of the quasi-market has been a concurrent polarisation in the market popularity of schools, based on, but reinforcing, previous trends.

This polarisation reaches into every aspect of school life. The school populations differ. Schools in wealthy areas have school populations dominated by middle-class *pakeha* (European New Zealand) people, and, increasingly wealthy Asian migrants. These students are characterised by a readiness to learn, quick adaption to the *habitus* of school life, relatively high levels of achievement, supportive two-parent families and relative stability.

The turnover of students in these schools tends to be low, a high proportion of 'voluntary' school donations are paid by parents, and there is scope for fundraising in the community (Gordon, 1993).

In the poorest areas, the school population is very different. More than half the families may exist on social welfare benefits, and those in work are generally in semi- or unskilled jobs. Maori and Pacific Island populations are much higher, as is the number of single-parent families. One clear characteristic is the transient nature of the population, as evidenced by one school in a recent study:

A large proportion of the school's population is relatively transient, hence the roll fluctuates a great deal and less than half of all pupils enrolled at the present time commenced their schooling at Bayview School. An additional factor influencing the transient nature of the School's population is the temporary enrolment of the children of women staying at refuges in the School's zone. (Quoted in Gordon, 1993, p. 5)

The issue of stability versus transience of population is one that has been highlighted in other research being undertaken in New Zealand (Lauder et al, 1994; Wood, 1995). A transient population leads to instability in a variety of ways educationally, organisationally and in terms of planning.

The extra educational problems caused by the differentiation of school populations is enhanced by differences in school governance. Boards of Trustees are all volunteers, but have a great deal of responsibility for running schools. There are no state-funded regional services to assist them in this task; if they wish to seek assistance, they must pay for it in the private sector. Board members reflect the catchment from which a school draws its students. In wealthy areas, this means that Board members will tend to have a high proportion of professional white-collar workers, who are quite used to running large enterprises. Many schools aim to ensure that their Boards include people with legal and accounting skills, to avoid having to pay professional fees (Gordon, 1993).

Schools in poor areas do not have access to the high levels of expertise available in wealthier areas. In one study (Gordon et al, 1994), the management of four schools – two rich, two poor, two primary and two secondary was directly compared. In the poor schools, school principals were forced to constantly explain issues to Board members, increasing the effort needed to make good decisions. Moreover, it was concluded that the actual decisions being made in the poor schools were notably harder and more complex, because of the difficulties caused by a market environment. In other words, there is a tendency towards an inverse relationship between the level of management expertise on school boards and the difficulty of the decisions that have to be made.

As the OECD (1994) notes, school choice in New Zealand has emerged as a phenomenon driven primarily by social rather than educational factors, although the difficulty in separating these cannot be overlooked. Examining this from a geopolitical perspective, Bronwyn Wood (1995) has concluded that, in a given market, the social location of a school is the best predictor of success in attracting students. Lauder et al (1994), in their examination of a specific secondary school market, found that school location and prior popularity were the key indicators of market success. Kauri College, which "has been at the 'bottom of the heap' for a long time according to local principals" (Lauder et al, 1994, p. 44), has almost halved its third form intake since 1990. On the other hand, Manuka College, "at the top of the local hierarchy" (1994, p. 50), was set to grow rapidly.

The relationship between socio-economic factors and changes to school rolls has to be explained in terms of the actual choices made by parents. Mike Fowler's (1993) study focuses on four schools in south and west Christchurch. He interviewed parents of children in their final year of full primary or intermediate schooling about their choices of secondary school. The crucial finding of Fowler's study is that decisions tend to be made by parents on criteria that are primarily social:

> *In choosing Lincoln over Hillmorton, 25 per cent of the ... comments made concerned Halswell parents' preferences for a "pleasant rural environment" and "fewer social problems" at Lincoln as against Hillmorton, which they saw as being in a "low socio-economic area" or in an "undesirable town environment" with "undesirable young people living in the area". In choosing Lincoln or Riccarton over Hornby, 28 per cent of the comments made by Branston parents also focused on Hornby's "low socio-economic area", "undesirable young people", "drugs" and "racial groups" and a "rough element". A socio-economic and social motive underpinned parent's reasons for considering schools which were further away. (Fowler, 1993, p. 108, my emphasis)*

In other words, patterns of school choice are *directly related* to the class and ethnic character of the area in which schools are located; the class effects noted above are not adventitious, but are central to education markets. These findings are similar to those of Waslander & Thrupp (1993), who, in an analysis of some of the Smithfield Project (Lauder et al, 1994) data, state:

> *In general terms our study has found that the concerns of market critics are justified. The choice to travel out of what was defined as the local zone prior to 1991 is more likely to be made by those from the upper end of each social stratum, irrespective of the ethnic background of the parents. Socio-economic segregation between schools has been exacerbated more than would be predicted simply on the basis of residential segregation. (Waslander & Thrupp, 1993, p. 31)*

Evidently, not all parents are empowered to make choices to move their children from unpopular schools. Some, as Fowler notes, stay in such schools because of a commitment to the concept of community schooling (1993, p. 108). It is those who seek social improvement who will tend to send their children further afield. As one parent commented in Fowler's study, she wished to "avoid my children mixing with others who haven't been brought up the same as mine" (1993, p. 109). Fowler also points out (ibid.) that those poorer schools which advertise themselves as being part of the community may be giving the entirely wrong message to attract those groups who precisely wish to escape their local community. Given the number of popular schools which are now full (and have become selective as a result), a further factor, that it is now schools, not parents, who often do the choosing, also needs to be taken into account.

A slightly different picture emerges from Wood's analysis of South Auckland schools; her 'market' included the area generally considered to be the most economically deprived in the country. Supporting Lauder et al's (1994) findings, Wood notes that secondary schools can be placed into two categories, according to whether their community is 'localised' or 'dispersed' (1995, pp. 54-57). Those schools which have a localised community tend to be those with falling rolls. Wood notes that very few students attend these schools from a distance of more than three kilometres (New Zealand cities are far less densely populated than British equivalents, and tend to sprawl further), the communities are characterised by a similarity of social and ethnic mixes, and they are chosen because they are the closest school.

Those with a 'dispersed' community exhibit very different characteristics. They have a much higher proportion of active 'choosers', students travel much further distances to reach these schools, and they tend to be selected primarily because of their actual or perceived academic success. Wood does not examine what happens to a dispersed school population once an enrolment scheme has been put in place to limit student numbers, and such a study has not yet been undertaken in New Zealand.

The effect of these patterns of parental choice is, as noted above, an increasing polarisation in the population, resources and positioning of schools. As schools at the bottom of the market hierarchy lose students to more popular schools, there are a number of negative effects. Most obvious is the immediate loss of funding, and a slightly delayed loss of staff. At the same time, the costs and resources associated with teaching those children who remain in the school are barely reduced at all. Whilst the toilet paper bill might decline, global resources such as heating, library books, school administration and class teaching materials are not reduced because of falling rolls (Gordon, 1993). Thus schools are precipitated into a crisis of funding.

At the same time, falling rolls apply pressure to schools to improve themselves so that future students can be attracted. Strategies such as improving the appearance of the premises, offering 'niche-marketed' programmes in the school, engaging in increased advertising or providing extra teachers or new teaching materials, are common. However, the costs of stopping or reversing roll decline are very large, and the likelihood of success for schools at the bottom of the market hierarchy is, on current evidence, minimal.

At the other end of the market hierarchy, successful schools have a different range of problems. Schools in this position have quickly become full, forcing them into enrolment schemes which limit the number of students in each intake. Enrolment schemes cut across and directly limit parental choice. Under enrolment schemes parents do not choose schools; schools choose students according to rules set out by the school. These rules are limited only by human rights legislation on discrimination. Two studies (Lauder et al, 1994 and Gordon et al, 1994) have examined the role of enrolment schemes. In Lauder et al's study, the local secondary school at the top of the hierarchy negotiated an early (1992) enrolment scheme with the Ministry. The aim was to cap the school roll at a figure far below original Ministry estimates of the school's capacity. Two reasons were given for this by the school's principal. The first was that, in his experience, smaller schools were better than larger schools. Secondly, the principal noted:

> *We were suddenly in the position of having absolutely no control over who came here and people came to the school with a range of educational problems for which we had no solutions because we had no special or discretionary staffing to deal with them. (Principal of Manuka College, quoted in Lauder et al., 1994, p. 50)*

Under the new enrolment scheme, the smallness of the school could be guaranteed. The Principal apparently believed that the enrolment scheme would also protect the school against those educational problems he discusses; the implication being that these are imported from outside of the immediate area of the school (and that they should be dealt with by other schools).

Lauder et al note that:

> *... since imposing a zone, (Manuka College's) exclusivity has intensified and its reputation consolidated. It has reinforced its dominant position in the local hierarchy and has become more competitive with the high SES schools further afield. (1994, p. 51)*

Whilst being full, and able to exert control over student numbers, has a number of advantages for schools, in a market environment it is not ideal. Markets require growth, not stagnation.

Market strategies are most evident in those schools which have intermediary positions between the extremes of the school spectrum. These schools have some relative space to position themselves in the marketplace because, especially at the secondary level, they tend to be in strategic locations, both in terms of geography and in relation to other close schools. They may, for example, be located on the boundary between quite wealthy middle-class areas and poorer ones, and will draw their students from both. Typically, students in the wealthier areas will attempt to enter more prestigious schools, but with increasing competition for places may end up (often slightly disgruntled) in the 'lesser' school. In market terms, the task for these schools is clear; to encourage a higher proportion of the wealthier children. It is at this point that the specific market strategies described in the next section become important, whether it be subject specialisation, new school uniforms, a change of 'image', tighter discipline, publicity or a variety of other factors (see Wood, 1995).

These intermediary schools also provide places for upwardly aspirant students from poorer areas which may also be close to the school, although such students may have to bypass a closer school which is lower on the market hierarchy. The balance of populations within the school is of constant concern. Too many working class or Maori children may discourage middle class parents (although this is usually expressed in terms of 'achievement', 'homework policy' or 'safety', not classism and racism), whilst it is crucial for the school to nurture its existing population; it could end up being deserted by all!

Market Image: the driving force of school choice

The principal of Otahuhu College commented that the choice of his schools for [academic] reasons was largely unsubstantiated in reality. He went on to comment that his school's School Certificate marks were in the bottom lower quartile of the country and certainly not as vastly superior to the Otara and Mangere schools as the parents think. (Wood, 1995, p. 79)

Cathy Wylie's (1994) survey makes the point that few New Zealand schools have responded to market pressures by changing their systems of curriculum or assessment; the most common response is to engage in advertising and other forms of promotion. This point is also made in the OECD's (1994) study of choice in six countries. Noting that it is notoriously difficult, even for academic researchers, to assess the academic impact of a school, the OECD says that "the atmosphere or ethos of the school seems to be at least as important", as 'situational' factors such as location (1994: 25). Thus the equation for success in attracting students appears to be 'location' (broadly conceived) plus 'image'. There is little that schools can do about locational factors. Their proximity to other schools, the class and ethnic mix of the area, even the name and prior reputation of the school, are hard to alter. Therefore, 'image', in all its forms, necessarily becomes the focus of change.

In New Zealand, as in other countries, the major focus of educational reform has been a claim that local management of schools, coupled with market competition, would assist schools to improve their educational 'product'. If a search for a new 'image' is the key market strategy employed by schools, we should be interested in the extent to which this contributes to substantive improvements in the delivery of education: is image underpinned by substance? There has, as yet, been inadequate research on this topic, but a number of points can be made.

Perhaps the most visible sign of school image is the students themselves, their dress and their behaviour. Most secondary schools have chosen to adopt school uniforms in the past, but in the post-reform era more attention than ever has been paid to school dress. It is, in market terms, a portable sign of corporate identity. A quite notable effect in one Auckland secondary school which chose not to have a school uniform is that students have deserted it for nearby schools in slightly poorer areas, reversing the usual finding of choice research (Timperley et al, 1992). Other schools which have resisted uniforms have, in recent times, introduced them. Many schools have invented a new uniform for the market age, usually reflecting the traditional 'grammar school' conservatism. As well, there is anecdotal evidence that schools are far more concerned to monitor students outside the school gate, as the uniform can be a highly visible marker of either desirable or unwanted behaviour.

Single-sex secondary schools, especially girls' schools, have generally become increasingly popular in the market environment, although no research has yet been done to find out why. There is, in many centres, a historical link between single-sex schools and academic achievement, which provides a partial explanation for the phenomenon. Most girls' schools were also built before the big post-war expansion of working class suburbs, and so tend to be located in 'good' areas. Another explanation is firmly linked to the issue of market image. Girls' schools are seen as academic in orientation and socially safe. In other words, these schools fit very closely the stated criteria of parents for a good school for their daughters. In the new market, being a single-sex girls' school is a big advantage.

Ethnic composition is a crucial indicator of school image. Schools with a high Maori or Pacific Island population have experienced significant white flight over the past few years (Wood, 1995), and most schools with a high non-*pakeha* population have experienced falling rolls as a result. The resulting ethnic segregation is colourfully illustrated in Lauder et al's study of one market. However, that study also demonstrated that, in an area with a high Maori population, schools are able to make a virtue out of catering to Maori students without losing students. One school was "developing an image as a bicultural school" (Lauder et al, 1994, p. 44), thereby maintaining a higher position in the local market than an adjacent school.

Image is as important to schools at the top of the local hierarchy as to those fighting for an increased market share. It is (partly) their image which got them to the top, and they jealously guard it. One way of doing this is to implement enrolment schemes which ensure that the current school population is reproduced or (socially and academically) enhanced. This, in a sense, happens naturally. It is boards of trustees who decide the nature of enrolment schemes, and these consist mainly of parents who are elected by parents to represent the current parental body (or that proportion which votes). Enrolment schemes often privilege children living in a set geographical area; and this may be drawn and redrawn to reflect the characteristics of the school's ideal student intake, presumably including those areas where trustees live. Other common forms of selection include interviews with parents and prospective students by the principal and board members. These selection techniques have led Hirsch (1995) to label boards of trustees in selective schools as 'self-perpetuating oligarchies', bent on reproducing their own image. Lauder et al (1994) note that the most socially just form of selection would appear to be a 'ballot', where students' names are drawn out one by one in random order.

Niche-marketing, which offers specialist courses or facilities to students is another common way in which schools have attempted to improve their market image. The sciences, music, drama and certain languages are popular additions to curricula of schools. Some image-making strategies are now universal: a glossy prospectus, attempts to get 'good news' stories into the media, open days at every opportunity, direct marketing into favoured junior schools and a generally high profile in local communities. Such things have, in many cases, been achieved at enormous cost, using funds which would otherwise provide teaching resources or library services to students. The irony of market image is that it may be achieved at the expense of real gains in the educational programmes of schools.

School image has become powerfully related to an idealised notion of private schooling, especially the English 'public' school, as it has in the United Kingdom. As Edwards & Whitty (1995) note, this prevents the development of a diverse schooling system, as most schools struggle to be identified with the powerful overriding image of the private. The private sector in New Zealand is quite small, and relatively few schools combine the traditional and academic characteristics of this ideal, but nevertheless the image is strong, and encouraged by Government policy. A version of the Assisted Places Scheme has recently been introduced, which offers the chance for a very limited number of low income families to 'escape' state schools and move into the private sector. As well, private schools are now paid a state subsidy of 50 percent of their teachers' salaries.

However, the drive to the private has gone further than mere approximations. State schools are now allowed, indeed encouraged, to market themselves to Asian countries in order to attract 'full fee-paying overseas students'. These are students whose families do not have residence in this country; they come here specifically to purchase educational services. Schools which are full are nevertheless able to take on 'extra' students if they pay full fees. Funding from this source can improve school programmes and also provide the basis for further expansion by the purchase of extra classrooms from the profit. Fees are set at around $7-8,000 (£3,000 approximately). Some schools may pull in upwards of 70 students, and thus half a million dollars! This educational market is well-organised, with school representatives travelling annually to a variety of Asian destinations to sell their product. No study has yet been done of this recent phenomenon.

Conclusion

New Zealand, as the state-of-the-art quasi-market schooling system in the English-speaking world, does not offer a very encouraging example for other countries to follow (Hirsch, 1995). The schools have never looked better. They have new signs, well-painted buildings and tidy grounds. The children have never looked better, decked out in their new uniforms and aware of the need to behave well on the streets. There is no problem in getting information about schools in order to make choices; parents are positively bombarded with it. But the quasi-market has brought with it a rapid growth in inequalities between schools, in terms of income, school population and the provision of resources for the future. Good education is now, more than ever, identified with schools in wealthy areas. At the other end, there seems little that schools at the bottom of the market hierarchy can do to improve their position. These schools often have a high incidence of truancy and serious behaviour problems, and no resources with which to solve it. The notion of *comparable quality* is dead, replaced with the (unwritten) message to compete or perish.

There appears to be no Ministerial defence of state schooling in New Zealand; indeed, there is some evidence that the Government has been considering the introduction of a voucher scheme (Smith, 1995) which would cut across both state and private schools, thereby undermining the former. It is a further way in which the Government can shed responsibility for the provision of education (see Friedman, 1962; Sexton, 1991). Nevertheless, the cost of such a scheme is likely to prevent its introduction, and the Ministry of Education has also warned of the further social injustice that would result (Ministry of Education, 1994).

The stated aim of school reform in New Zealand was to improve the quality of education in the state sector. There is no evidence at all that this has happened (OECD, 1994), or indeed how competition could translate into school improvement (given the critiques of Chubb & Moe's 1990 analysis). What has improved greatly is the ability of schools to make choices over how to spend their funds, and that aspect of the reforms is strongly supported (Wylie, 1994). The cost of this has been the devolution of responsibility to volunteer boards of trustees, teachers and, especially, school principals. Also, in many schools, budget-setting is less a choice between competing options than trying to squeeze the essentials out of an inadequate budget. There are now a large number of schools posting annual deficits, which possibly heralds a major flaw in the funding system. It is unlikely that the Ministry would cut off funds to an overdrawn school, although warning letters are frequently sent to schools.

The future of New Zealand's education quasi-market is far from clear at this point. Each further withdrawal of the state has left education as a site of contested terrain (Jessop et al, 1990), wherein forces both for and against the neo-liberal agenda fight for control, against a backdrop of the increased primacy of private over public interests. It is somewhat ironic, however, that each shift towards the private is accompanied by increasing regulatory powers in the public sector, leaving the state as a residual force but also as a necessary, continued presence in the 'business' of schooling. The quasi-market policy thus remains highly contradictory, and the resolution of these contradictions increasingly problematic.

Notes

[1] This trend has recently been reversed. See Elley, 1994.

[2] This is not because the state has been reluctant to devolve this funding, but due to the very successful campaigns against the devolution of teacher salaries, supported by teacher unions and boards of trustees; see OECD, 1994; Gordon, 1994.

References

Bartlett, W. (1993) Quasi-markets and educational reforms, in J. Le Grand & W. Bartlett (Ed.) *Quasi-Markets and Social Policy*. London: Macmillan.

Chubb, J. & Moe, T. (1990) *Politics, Markets and America's Schools*. Washington: Brookings Institute.

Dale, R. (1989) *The State and Education Policy*. Milton Keynes: Open University Press.

Dale, R. & Ozga, J. (1993) Two hemispheres – both new right? 1980s education reform in New Zealand and England and Wales, in B. Lingard, J. Knight & P. Porter (Eds) *Schooling Reform in Hard Times*. London: Falmer.

Edwards, T. & Whitty, G. (1995) Marketing quality: traditional and modern versions of educational excellence. Paper presented at AERA Conference, San Francisco, April.

Elley, W. (1994) *The IEA Study of Reading Literacy*. Oxford: Pergamon Press.

Fowler, M. (1993) *Factors Influencing Choice of Secondary School: a case study*. Christchurch: University of Canterbury.

Friedman, M. (1962) *Capitalism and Freedom*. Chicago: University of Chicago Press.

Gamble, A. (1988) *The Free Economy and the Strong State*. London: Macmillan.

Glennerster, H. (1991) Quasi-markets and education, *Economic Journal*, 101, pp. 1268-1271.

Gordon, L. (1992) The state, devolution and educational reform in New Zealand, *Journal of Education Policy*, 7, pp. 187-203.

Gordon, L. (1993) *A Study of Boards of Trustees in Canterbury Schools*. Christchurch: Education Policy Research Unit.

Gordon, L., Boyask, D. & Pearce, D. (1994) *Governing Schools: a comparative analysis*. Christchurch: Education Policy Research Unit.

Hayek, F.A. (1991) *Economic Freedom*. London: Institute of Economic Affairs.

Hills, J. (1995) *Inquiry into Income and Wealth, volume two*. York: Joseph Rowntree Foundation.

Hirsch, D. (1995) The other school choice: how oversubscribed schools select their students. Paper presented in a public lecture at London Institute of Education, May.

Hood, C. (1995) *Explaining Economic Policy Reversal.* Buckingham: Open University Press.

Jessop, B., Bonnett, K. & Bromley, S. (1990) Farewell to Thatcherism? Neo-liberalism and 'new times', *New Left Review*, 179, pp. 81-102.

Joseph Rowntree Foundation (1995) *Inquiry into Income and Wealth.* York: Joseph Rowntree Foundation.

Lauder, H., Hughes, D., Waslander, S., Thrupp, M., McGlinn, J., Newton, S. & Dupuis, A. (1994*) The Creation of Market Competition for Education in New Zealand: an empirical analysis of a New Zealand secondary school market, 1990-1993.* Wellington: Ministry of Education.

Le Grand, J. (1991) Quasi-markets and social policy, *Economic Journal*, 101, pp. 1256-1267.

Ministry of Education (New Zealand) (1994) *Education Vouchers in the School Sector.* Discussion Paper. Wellington: Government Printer.

Nozick, R. (1974) *Anarchy, State and Utopia.* New York: Basic Books.

OECD (1994) *School: a matter of choice.* Paris: OECD.

Pusey, M. (1991) *Economic Rationalism in Canberra.* Melbourne: Cambridge University Press.

Saunders, P. (1994) Rising on the Tasman tide: income inequality in New Zealand and Australia in the 1980s, *Social Policy Journal of New Zealand*, 2, pp. 97-113.

Sexton, S. (1991) *New Zealand Schools.* Wellington: New Zealand Business Roundtable.

Smith, L. (1995) The New Zealand experience. Speech notes for conference on charter schools, November.

Timperley, H., McNaughton, S., Parr, J. & Robinson, V. (1992) *Community-School Collaboration: beliefs and practices.* Auckland: Auckland Uniservices Ltd.

Treasury, The (New Zealand) (1987) *Briefing Paper to the Incoming Government, Volume II: education issues.* Wellington: Government Printer.

Waslander, S. & Thrupp, M. (1993) Choice, competition and segregation: an empirical analysis of a secondary school market 1990-1993. Unpublished paper.

Wilson, K. (1991) The Picot Report and the legitimation of education policy. Unpublished M.Ed.Admin. thesis, Massey University.

Wood, B. (1995) The geo-politics of school choice: Auckland secondary school selection. Unpublished MA thesis, Geography Department, University of Auckland.

Wylie, C. (1994) *Self-managing Schools in New Zealand: the fifth year.* Wellington: New Zealand Council for Educational Research.

Notes on Contributors

Peter W. Cookson, Jr, is Director of Educational Outreach and Extension, Teachers College Columbia University. He is the author of many journal articles and has written or edited nine books, including *School Choice: the struggle for the soul of American education*; *Choosing Schools: vouchers and American education* (with Jerome J. Hanus); and *Preparing for Power: America's élite boarding schools* (with Caroline Hodges Persell). He is currently writing a book about educational policy-making at the federal level. In 1993 he was the American Sociological Association's Congressional Fellow in the United States Senate.

Liz Gordon is a Senior Lecturer in Educational Policy at the University of Canterbury, New Zealand. Her primary interest is in the role of the state in relation to educational policy. In recent years she has focused on the effects of devolution of responsibility, school choice and the growth of educational quasi-markets, both in New Zealand and internationally. She has published articles in a number of journals, including the *Journal of Education Policy, British Journal of Sociology of Education, Educational Policy, Comparative Education* and the *New Zealand Journal of Educational Studies*. At present, she is working on a book entitled *Changing Markets in Education*, to be published by the Open University Press. She is also actively involved in politics, acting as education spokesperson for the Alliance, a coalition of political parties opposed to new right reforms.

Sjoerd Karsten is Associate Professor of Educational Policy and Administration and Director of the Centre for the Study of Educational Policy and Organization at the University of Amsterdam. His research centres on local educational policy and administration. He has published on local governments, the teaching profession, ethnic segregation, and comparative education. He recently co-edited the volume entitled *Education in East Central Europe: educational changes after the fall of communism.*

Simon Marginson is a Senior Lecturer at the Centre for the Study of Higher Education at the University of Melbourne and chairs the Editorial Board of *Australian Universities Review*. He is author of *Education and Public Policy in Australia* (Cambridge 1993) and other publications and reports on higher education, schooling, vocational education and labour market issues. He recently completed a doctorate on education markets, and a history of Australian education titled *For all of us? Government, education and citizenship in Australia since 1960* (forthcoming).

Gary Miron is a researcher and Director of Studies at Stockholm University's Institute of International Education. He has written a number of articles and books on such topics as special needs education, educational evaluation, and the restructuring of education. Over the past three years he has conducted research and written on the topic of educational restructuring in Sweden. In addition to this more theoretical work, he has obtained practical experience with this topic by participating in the establishment of two independent pre-schools. He is currently working on two research projects with colleagues that deal with restructuring: one covers a number of case countries in Europe and the other examines the changes taking place in Guinea-Bissau and Nicaragua.

Brigitte Steinert studied educational science and sociology and received a doctorate in educational science at the University of Frankfurt am Main. She is Research Associate in the Department of Economics of Education at the German

Institute for International Educational Research in Frankfurt am Main. Her main research topics are: educational planning and policy, sociology of education, development in educational research. She is author and co-author of several articles including: Case studies of innovation in educational research and development: Germany, in *Educational Research and Development: trends, issues and challenges* (Paris, OECD/CERI, 1995); Educational research in the Federal Republic of Germany, in *Educational Research and Development: Austria, Germany, Switzerland* (Paris, OECD, 1995); Markt und Privatisierung im Bildungsbereich: Internationale Tendenzen, Tertium Comparationis, *Journal für Internationale Bildungsforschung* (1996) (with M. Weiss).

Christine Teelken studied Organizational Management at the University of Groningen, the Netherlands, and education at the University of York, United Kingdom. She is preparing a dissertation about school choice and organizational features of schools in an international comparative perspective at the University of Amsterdam. Her research comprises England, Scotland and the Netherlands. Previously, she published on competition between schools in the United States of America and the Netherlands. She works part-time for a management consultancy firm.

Agnès van Zanten is a Researcher in Sociology at the Centre National de la Recherche Scientifique (France). She prepared her Master's degree at Stanford (USA) and obtained her doctorate at La Sorbonne Paris V University. She has published several books and articles on urban education, parents and schools, local educational policies and politics, the schooling of immigrant children and sociological and anthropological traditions in education. She is at present conducting a comparative British-French research project on markets, diversity and choice with Stephen Ball, Meg Maguire and Sheila Macrae from King's College, University of London.

Geoffrey Walford is Lecturer in Educational Studies (sociology) in the Department of Educational Studies, University of Oxford and is a Fellow of Green College, Oxford. He was previously Senior Lecturer in Sociology and Education Policy at Aston Business School, Aston University, Birmingham. He is author of many academic articles and book chapters, and author or editor of 15 books. These include: *Life in Public Schools* (Methuen, 1986); *Restructuring Universities: politics and power in the management of change* (Croom Helm, 1987); *Privatization and Privilege in Education* (Routledge, 1990); *City Technology College* (Open University Press, 1991)(with Henry Miller); *Choice and Equity in Education* (Cassell, 1994) and *Educational Politics: pressure groups and faith-based schools* (Avebury, 1995).

Manfred Weiss is Senior Researcher in the Department of Economics of Education at the German Institute for International Educational Research in Frankfurt am Main and Lecturer at the College of Education in Erfurt. He received a doctorate in economics from the Technical University, Berlin. In 1987 he was a visiting professor at the State University of New York at Buffalo. His main research interests involve the economics of education, educational planning and policy, and international developments in education. Recent publications include: Der Arbeitsplatz Universität und die Zukunft der Hochsculen (with B von Kopp), in J. Enders & K. Teichler (Eds) *Der Hochschullehrerberuf* (Luchterhand, Neuwied); Mikroökonomie der Schule, in H.G. Rolff (Ed.) *Zukunftsfelder von Schulforschung* (Weinheim, Deutscher Studienverlag, 1995); Bildungsökonomische Wirkungsforschung: Konzepte, Methoden, empirische Befunde, in U.P. Trier (Ed.) *Wirksamkeitsanalyse von Bildungssystemen* (Bern und Aarau, 1995).